THE ART OF LIVING

Ross Brittleton

"How can anyone live without being instructed in the art of living and dying?

Meister Eckhart

The Art of Living

ISBN: 978-0-9556367-4-5

Published by Anchor Print Group Ltd

Published in Great Britain by the Anchor Print Group Ltd

First edition published in 2009

Contents

INTRODUCTION — 7
    'A Life Frozen in time' — 12
    Tools — 14
    Needs — 14

Portrait of a person who 'manages' life effectively — 16

The Wheel of Change — 18

Notes of doing exercises — 20

— 21

SELF MANAGEMENT
'Know Thyself'

Where Am I now?   Life Situation Assessment — 21

Learning How To Relax — 23
    Breathing — 24
    Muscle tension/relax — 24
    Count down induction — 25

Emotions — 27
    Recognising Emotions — 27
    Charting strength and frequency of emotions — 28
    Habits for responding to feelings — 29

Values — 33
    Personal values — 34
    Societal values — 35
    Opposing values — 36
    How strong are your values — 39
    Patterns of change — 39

Boundaries — 41
    Defining Roles & Boundaries — 41
    Developing Boundaries — 43
    Managing Role Conflicts — 44

Metaphor — 47
    Change through metaphor — 49
    Metaphors and stories — 49
    "The wind and the sun" — 50

Power Of Beliefs   53

Separating beliefs and opinions   53
Challenging your belief system   54
How to challenge harmful beliefs and false assumptions   56

Optimist Or Pessimist?   59

Methods Of Motivation   63

Visualisation (using the imagination)
Practising the task in imagination   69
Anticipate difficulties   69

PEOPLE SKILLS

Communicating Effectively   71
Communicating Effectively   71
Communication Style   71
Developing Effective Communication Skills   75

The 'Eye' Factor   80
The four skills involved in the Visual or Eye Factor: 81
Eyes Communication   81
Posture and Movement   82
Developing Physical Awareness   85
Fundamental Principles   86
Breathing   86
Posture/Alignment   87
Stretching/ Movement   88
Concentration   89
Discipline   89
Dress and appearance   90
Gestures and Smiles   92
Developing Gestures   93

The 'Energy' Factor   94
Circle of Attention   94
Physcial Attending   95
Level I Listening   96
Level II Listening   97
Level III Listening   98
Voice   100
Four basic components of voice   101

Words - 'Vague' Language   102
Words, non words, the pause and silence   105
Humour.   109

Self Development Of The 'Emotional Centre'   110

           Fear   111
           Public Speaking   114

Other Factors   Feedback   118
           Video feedback   119
           Self-awareness   120
           Disparity   120
           Mental agility   121
           Trust Your Mind   122
           Confidence Equals Mastery   123

8 Steps To Transform Your Skills   124

GOALS

Setting Goals   129
           Life Situation Assessment   129
           Goals Exercise   130
           S.M.A.R.T.E,R. Goals   131
           Develop a strategy for change   135

The Observing Self   139
           Accessing the observing self   140
           Questions and actions that help   140
           Statements   140
           Behavioural example   141
           Imaginative example   141

Things Not To Do   143

Things To Do   146

ADDITIONAL RESOURCES

Seeking help   148

Life Situation Assessment   150

Life Situation Assessment Logsheet   151

Complaint, Criticism or Contempt   153

Success Patterning   161

The Autonomic Nervous System   162

Habits for Responding To Feelings   168

References   170

Bibliography   172

"A man without awareness is like a carriage whose passengers are the desires, with the muscles for horses, while the carriage itself is the skeleton. Awareness is the sleeping coachman. As long as the coachman remains asleep the carriage will be dragged aimlessly here and there. Each passenger seeks a different destination and the horses pull different ways. But when the coachman is wide awake and holds the reins the horses will pull the carriage and bring every passenger to his proper destination"

Tibetan Parable

Introduction

"Any significant change demands deep, revolutionary modification in our attitude and response. It is possible to form individuals capable of coping with a changing world without such intense emotional upheavals that bring many to breakdowns."

Moshe Feldenkrais

Do you believe that 'living effectively' is an art? If your answer to that question is yes then it follows that you will recognise that to live effectively knowledge, enthusiasm, skill and effort are all required. To learn any 'art' also needs patience, persistence, concentration and discipline. This book is based on the assumption that living effectively is indeed an 'art' and attempts to give the reader the opportunity to practise and develop the necessary skills that will help them to be more effective in all aspects of their life.

Whether we like it or not, whether we want it to or not, life happens. Our bodies, our lives, our environment and the world we live in are in a constant process of change. We can blindly accept this process, deny it, try to control it or learn how to manage our lives in an effective way.

Life happens and in order to live more effectively, to manage problems that may occur and to take advantage of any opportunities that may present themselves we all need a range of skills and the ability to manage our lives and the changes that occur. This does not mean that we accept all changes in our lives without question. Whenever considering any change it is wise to take time to consider the benefits and the costs of that change in personal, physical, social and environmental terms. Those who suggest changing aspects of our lives would, I suggest, benefit from taking the time to convince all concerned that any such change will eventually improve the quality of our lives and ultimately benefit all concerned.

We live in a world in which we are constantly reminded by the news and other media that more and more people are experiencing difficulty with living effectively. Mental health problems are becoming an ever increasing problem and articles appear on a regular basis that outline the scale of the problem. *"80 million working days are lost in the UK each year as a result of stress, anxiety and depression."* A study based on 245,000 people living and working in the UK concluded that *"depression can do more physical damage to a person's health than several long-term diseases"* ("The Guardian" 7th September 2007). Over 2 million people in the UK are currently on incapacity benefit. Mental health issues touch everyone from all walks of life and in all professions. It is also estimated that only 1 in 4 people who are experiencing mental health problems seek help.

From the above it appears clear that many people are obviously struggling with managing their lives and suffering from some form of emotional or mental distress and need help. We will all come into contact with people experiencing emotional or mental distress at some point or other in their lives. So, one might reasonably ask why these things happen and how do we equip ourselves with the necessary knowledge and skills so that we can learn to live more effectively.

Success in all areas of life and work is based on a combination of many factors. The most obvious is that you choose a career and pursue the necessary training so that you can earn a living. It is also important, and not so obvious, that you be passionate and enthusiastic about your chosen 'path', have clear goals, develop the skills and abilities needed in life and work, develop self-confidence and eventually, when all of this is put together you will be in a position to bring out the best in yourself and others.

I hope it is clear from the above that there are many factors, 'forces' or 'barriers' that influence our ability to manage our lives effectively. In order to overcome these 'barriers' people need to know how to identify the 'barriers' that will prevent their development and to develop the 'skills' required which will give them the chance to make the most of the opportunities that life will present them. Everyday and every week people fail to get the best out of themselves and perform to the best of their abilities. So, one might reasonably ask several questions:

- What stops people living more effectively?
- Why don't people seek help?

- What approach or approaches will help most?
- Who will help most?

What stops people living more effectively? There are numerous theories as to why people experience difficulties in living their lives effectively and have trouble in their lives. Many of these theories will, in one way or another focus on one or more of the factors described below. The key factors affecting our ability to live effectively are:

Learned Patterns of Behaviour (Habits) – Throughout our lives we learn many things and this will include ways of behaving, a value system and a belief system. Through constant repetition and reinforcement this learning eventually passes into our unconscious and we develop ways of doing things and thinking. In short, all of this learning becomes habitual. We are all creatures of habit and we tend to do things in the same way day in day out. Habits can be of great value if they help a person to live more effectively but problems occur when habitual responses no longer serve a purpose and this can ultimately lead to difficulties being encountered in living causing distress for the individual and others around them.

The use or mis-use of our 'innate' resources We have many 'resources' and these include our awareness, imagination, a complex brain that allows us to think things through, the ability to establish rapport and develop empathy. However these 'resources' can work against us. Take for example our imagination. In a given situation we can imagine many outcomes but if we frequently imagine the worst-case scenario our imagination is working against our best interests and how we think can have a tremendous impact on how we approach and deal with the many challenges we meet throughout life.

Whether or not certain perceived '*needs*' are being met. Maslow was one of the first to introduce the 'hierarchy of needs' and how important the meeting of these needs was to our well-being and development. Ideas on these 'needs' have developed over the years and 'needs' can essentially be split into two types: **Primary Needs** which include the need for include the need for *food, clothing, a roof over your head* and the *need for stimulation* and **Secondary Needs,** which are determined by social and cultural influences, and include *security, fun, purpose, control, intimacy, connection and a sense of belonging.*

If one, or more of these needs goes unmet for a long period of time then there is an increasing risk that this will affect a person's ability to live their lives effectively.

The *'emotional state'* of a person. Our emotional state has an enormous impact on every aspect of our lives. When someone is in a highly emotional state they usually respond in one of three ways. **Fight, flight or freeze.** In the **fight** reaction they will probably be confrontational, aggressive or argumentative. In **flight** they will probably run away from a difficult or threatening situation and in the **freeze** you will probably find people who become very defensive, rigid, or be incapable of making a decision. It is generally agreed that it is difficult, if not impossible, for a person in a highly emotional state to think logically and so handle a situation in a rational way and if they don't learn to manage their emotional state they will lose control and experience 'distress' in their lives and their health and their quality of life will suffer.

Skills and Capabilities. In order to be successful in your personal or professional life or in any activity you decide to undertake you need to reach a level of skill and be capable of performing at a certain level. This will enable you to develop relationships, earn a living, perform an activity to a desired level and have some success in your personal and professional lives.

People also need to be able to manage their emotions, manage relationships, communicate effectively and be properly trained to do the work they have chosen to do. If a person lacks the relevant skills or abilities to meet the demands of their chosen career or life's challenges then it is highly likely they will experience difficulties which could be physical, emotional or psychological and their lives will suffer.

On top of these factors we live in a fast-moving, ever-changing society and culture in which people are facing increasing demands and temptations. For many this becomes too much to cope with and their performance inevitably suffers.

Why don't people seek help? At times it may be necessary to accept we can't do it all on our own and it may be necessary to seek help from family, a friend, a mentor or a professional. Many people do seek help but many others don't and perhaps it's worthwhile considering why so many people are reluctant to seek help or advice.

There are several reasons people don't seek help and these are:

- It is not easy to receive help
- It is difficult to commit one's self to change
- It is difficult to submit to the influence of someone else: help can be seen as a threat to esteem, integrity, and independence.
- It is not easy to trust others you may know or a stranger and be open with them.
- It is not easy to see one's problems clearly at first.
- It's difficult to admit to having a problem
- Sometimes problems seem too large, too overwhelming, or too unique to share easily.
- Cost – people may be unable or unwilling to pay the physical, psychological or financial 'price' for help

All of these are reasons used for not seeking help but the long-term consequences of not seeking help are a life that can be filled with anxiety, distress, depression and many physical problems that are related to stress. Many of these problems are, in many cases, avoidable if a person seeks 'skilled help' or takes steps towards prevention sooner, rather than later.

What approach or approaches will help most? There are hundreds of theories and approaches about motivation and the best way to help people. All of these approaches have a common core and that is *'problem management and opportunity development'*. In short there are two ends on the scale and these are 'non-directive' and 'directive'. The non-directive approach involves someone who will mainly listen whilst you talk and the idea is that through talking you will eventually gain 'insight' into your problems and resolve them. On the other end of the scale is the 'directive' approach. The 'directive' approach is very goal focused and means you will be given lots of advice and suggestions. When considering the best approach for you it is a good idea to have some awareness of the kind of approaches mentioned above and what you will respond to best.

Who will help most? Research has consistently shown that one of the most important factors in the effectiveness of any form of 'helping, coaching, training or counselling' is the relationship between the 'helper' and the 'helpee.' So, if you are seeking help for yourself or others it is very important that you as the 'helpee' feel comfortable with the person helping you. The next thing you need to look at is the approach used by the 'helper'. I would offer the view that the 'skilled helper' will adopt an 'eclectic' approach and design their approach around what will suit the individual best. Essentially they will look at the five areas mentioned above and address **'habits'**, the use or mis-use of **'innate resources'**, assess whether **'needs'** are being met and also identify which **'skills'** are needed to help manage the **'emotional condition'** more effectively. People may need help with one or more of these and, in my opinion, the 'skilled helper' will be able to help with all of these areas.

Can I help myself? There are, in my view, many things people can do to help themselves and the purpose of this book is to share some of the techniques and knowledge that can be used.

You may be reading this book because you've decided that you're not quite happy with the way your life is and you'd like to make some changes. Or perhaps you do want to or maybe you have to make some changes but you're not quite sure how to go about it. Or, you've tried to make some changes and they've not turned out exactly as you'd expected and you find yourself back at square one and you're not sure whether it's worth the effort to try again.

Whatever your reasons for reading this book the aim is to give you the knowledge and tools you need to help you find a way to live your life effectively. Whether you want to develop self-confidence, deal with emotional difficulties, break destructive habits, improve your self-esteem, communicate more effectively or develop your emotional or social intelligence this book contains materials that will help you.

Perhaps, like many others, you think that changing part or all of your life is too difficult for you or that you don't need to change. If you have any doubts about the need to manage change effectively then consider what a life frozen in time would be like…

A life frozen in time

If you wanted to keep your life exactly the same as it is now, how would you do it? What would you do to stay in the same frame of mind? Work at the same job, keep the same relationships, do the same everything? How would you avoid meeting influential new people – become a recluse? How would you stop learning new information – stop reading the papers and watching the news? How would you keep yourself from trying new things? The things you want to do or have are most likely possible, but not if you continue to do the same things in the same ways.

Yapko

As mentioned earlier this book contains ideas and methods based on over 25 years of my experience and research in the arts, education, business and health. A complete list of authors I have drawn upon can be found in the bibliography but I will mention here some of the most important ones. They include, *Seligman*[1], *Goleman*[2], *Cutter*[3], *Griffin*[4], *Beck*[5], *Schumacher*[6], *Semler*[7], *Dalai Lama*[8], *Argyle*[9], *Feldenkrais*[10], *Berry*[11], *Stanislawski,*[12] *Egan*[13] and *Yapko*[14]. The methods used are based on a wide variety of approaches from many different sources including writers in psychology, education, philosophy, the arts and sociology. Many people believe that personal development always works best when coming from a *real* understanding of what it is to be a human being. This approach draws its power from observation, research, experience, the biological and psychological sciences and our heritage of wisdom gathered down the ages. For change and development to be effective we have to be aware, not only of the requirement for physical and emotional security, but of the 'tools' that we have available and others that we have acquired during our lives that we use for understanding and impacting on our environment. When used well, they can provide purpose, achievement and good emotional and mental well-being; when not developed or used wrongly, they cause misery and difficulties.

Yapko[15] suggests that there are three key areas that people need skills in to live effectively and manage whatever changes they experience. The first of these areas relates to yourself, your thought processes, your values, your emotional management, your belief systems and the ability to use the 'tools/resources' at your disposal. In short your **'intrapersonal skills'** or, if you prefer, how well you know yourself or **'self-awareness'**.

The second area is your ability to relate to others in the world around you and the skills you need to communicate effectively and develop relationships with others. Your **'interpersonal'** or 'people skills'.

Finally there is your **'behaviour'** or what you do. For this reason the book is divided into three sections dealing with developing 'self-awareness', your inner processes and 'tools/resources' first and then your communication or 'people skills'. Finally we look at the 'goal setting' process and putting the 'theory' into practise.

By working with the ideas given in this book, living, managing change and development is more effective because it takes into account *many different* aspects of what we know about what a human being actually is. Fortunately none of us starts with a blank canvas or an 'empty toolbox'. Our genetic inheritance, our education, the skills we have learned throughout our lives, the society in which we live, our family, friends, work colleagues and environment provide us with a wealth of information and 'tools'. The 'tools' we have include:

Tools

- The different functions of brain hemispheres
- The functions of the emotional mind (limbic system)
- The role of trance in human behaviour and problematic states
- The role of imagination in generating and solving psychological problems
- The recognition that the healing response is a rich system of mind/body communication
- The physical attributes of the body
- The ability to communicate
- The ability, on occasion, to make free choices in life - free will
- The importance of the 'Observing Self' and how to use it to separate the core identity of a person from his or her problem
- The differences between male and female approaches to thinking, feeling and communication

14

Needs

As we go through childhood, to our teenage years and eventually into adulthood we are taught and learn that living effectively also involves the meeting of certain 'needs'. These **'needs'** can be divided into two types. **Primary Needs** which are considered essential for our survival and **Secondary Needs** which are largely determined by social and cultural influences and how we meet these secondary needs will have a large impact on how we live our lives and determine what is success.

Primary Needs

- The need for food
- The need for clothes to wear
- The need for a roof over your head
- The need for stimulation and learning

Secondary Needs

- The need for security
- The need for fun, pleasure and intimacy
- The need to dream
- The role of each individual's search for meaning
- The need for autonomy and to feel in control over one's environment
- The need for attention - to give and receive it - in all human interaction and how the attention interchange is essential for stabilising human communities
- We learn there is a need for a sense of community and a need to make a contribution to the wider community
- The need for status

When we take into account as many aspects as possible of what it is to be human then learning to live life more effectively is more likely to be swift and inevitable.

If you've decided to make any changes in your life then you can see from the above that you already have a great number of 'tools' at your disposal and that many of the 'needs' that you want to be met have been identified and are common to us all.

Portrait of a person who manages live effectively

> *"Suit the action to the word the word to the action with this special observance. that you o'erstep not the modesty of nature."*

Hamlet

Some people seem to live far more effectively than others. They manage 'problems' more easily and they are also able to develop and take advantage of any opportunities that present themselves. Many would call this 'luck', or put it down to genetics or social and economic reasons. Whatever the reasons I believe that truly successful people are successful and happy because they are 'mature adults'. In normal human development we can say that we go through three distinct stages of development. As a child we are completely **dependent** on adults to support us and help us through life. As we develop we move into an **independent** phase where we start to make our own choices and break away from the influence of our parents and other adults. Finally as we grow, develop and mature we move into an **inter-dependent** phase where, hopefully, we realise that we are all inter-dependent on each other. In order to facilitate the movement through these phases a range of tasks have been identified that need to be accomplished in moving from dependence to independence and interdependence. All of them require, directly or indirectly, a bias toward action in life. *Egan*[1] offers the view that an effective person act in the following ways:

- Assumes an active rather than a passive role in life. In a word is 'pro-active'.

- Changes from a state of dependency on others to relative independence and then recognise the importance and value of interdependence.

- Widens their range of behaviours. Act in many rather than few ways.

- Develops a wider range of interests – moving from erratic, shallow, and casual interests to mature, strong, and enduring interests.

- Changes from a present-oriented time perspective to a perspective encompassing past, present, and future.

- Moves from solely subordinate relationships with others to relationships as equals or superiors.

- Changes from merely understanding theirself to some kind of control over their destiny.

This then, illustrates the qualities of a person who manages life and the changes that are faced effectively. The following chapters deal not only with the ideal but also with what is minimally necessary in order to get the best out of yourself and your life "for better" rather than "for worse."

The Wheel Of Change – Decision Wheel[15]

"People often fail to derive all the benefits of any method of readjustment, because they want to both change themselves and at the same time remain as they are."

Feldenkrais

If you have decided to take the steps necessary to live your life 'more effectively' it will probably mean making some changes in various aspects of your life. Making changes and the process of change is something that we all have to go through. Some find it easy, some not so easy and some find it difficult. So, you'll be pleased to know that everyone goes through the same process and what you and others experience is perfectly natural.

The change process and the decision making process has several stages to it and understanding this process will help you understand and manage the process more effectively:

1. You become **aware** of an issue or set of issues. For instance, not just this marital problem, but vague dissatisfaction with the relationship itself, or dissatisfaction with your job or social life.

2. A **sense of urgency** develops, especially as the problem situation becomes more annoying or difficult. This and the first step make up **consciousness-raising** stage of the process.

3. You begin to **look for solutions**. Different strategies for managing the problem situation are explored. For example, in the case of relationship difficulties: complaining openly, separating, getting a divorce, revenge, affairs, counselling and so on and so on. Or, in the case of a job: complaining, arriving late for work, loss of motivation, looking at the jobs section in the paper.

4. The **costs of choosing different solutions** begin to emerge. *"If I confront openly I'll have to go through the agony of confrontation, denial, argument, counter-accusation."* The possibilities are endless and people often retreat or give up because there is no cost-free or painless way of dealing with the problem and making the changes you want to make.

5. Since the problem situation is now seen for what it is, it is impossible to retreat and so **a more serious weighing of choices** takes place. Costs of confronting versus costs of withdrawing. Often, a kind of dialogue goes on in the person's mind between steps 4 and 5.

6. An **intellectual decision** is made to accept some choice and pursue a certain course of action. However a merely intellectual decision is often not enough to drive action.

7. The **heart joins the head** in the decision. The decision is reinforced by values and emotion and so this 'fuller' decision is more likely to drive action.

8. **Maintaining** change is then the next stage of the process.

9. Whenever anyone decides to make a change it is not uncommon for there to be a **relapse** or a **falling back** into the previous undesired behaviour. It is perhaps wise to remember that **relapse** is not failure. Relapse merely indicates to you that there is a weakness in your strategy and you may need to re-examine the steps you have taken so far and introduce new strategies.

Ideally you will move through this change process and there will be no **relapse**. If you hit a problem when changing all or part of your life then it's worth remembering that change is a process and you may hit obstacles or challenges or you may make mistakes at any point in this process. If, for example, you consider the 'costs' outweigh the 'benefits' then you'll probably go back to stage 3 and look at alternative solutions.

Notes on using the exercises outlined in this book.

"In all human functions that need apprenticeship, such as love, hatred, speaking, thinking, walking, sitting, and others no part of the apprenticeship can be skipped with complete impunity... making mistakes is essential to satisfactory learning. ...

Feldenkrais

The exercises in this book can be done in any order you choose. If you want to start with a particular section then please feel free to do so. However, it would be helpful if you do all the exercises in the book and take the time to review what you have written on a regular basis. This is not meant to be the kind of book you read once and once only. To get the best from this book you need to revisit what you have done and repeat the exercises if you feel it is necessary to do so.

A few hints may help you to make best use of the exercises in this book:

1. Take time. Devote some undisturbed period of time to an exercise. Even if this is only five minutes, make sure it is a time of its own, uninterrupted by other disturbances.

2. Prepare. Try and make sure you are in a relaxed frame of mind.

3. Spend enough time on an exercise so that you get maximum benefit from it.

4. Connect. After you have worked through an exercise remind yourself of what you did throughout the day or week. Spend a little time reflecting on an exercise you have done or a section you have read.

5. Work in silence. Sharing your results and thoughts too soon with people who may not understand them often reduces the benefits you have gained.

6. You may also want to keep a workbook in which to write about your experiences and keep a record of the changes that take place.

7. Always remember that you are in a 'learning process' and you are not expected to get everything 'right'.

SELF – MANAGEMENT

Where Am I Now?

Before you can decide where you are going or where you would like to be it is useful to have some idea of where you are. One of the simplest ways to give you a general idea of where you are in the major areas of you're your life is to complete the 'Life Situation Assessment' exercise below. This will give you a quick snap-shot of your life situation as it is now and can also be used to give you an idea of the areas in your life that you'd like to work on.

Life Situation Assessment

Use a scoring system from 1 to 10 (10 being the optimum score), that reflects your personal fulfilment, contentment, happiness and overall satisfaction with your present situation. It also gives you an indicator as to how well these general needs are being met at the present time. Address each area briefly and select a score based on your initial feelings.

	Low									High
• Health – Quality of Food	1	2	3	4	5	6	7	8	9	10
Amount of Food	1	2	3	4	5	6	7	8	9	10
Amount of Exercise	1	2	3	4	5	6	7	8	9	10
• Personal Growth	1	2	3	4	5	6	7	8	9	10
• Work/Career	1	2	3	4	5	6	7	8	9	10
• Financial	1	2	3	4	5	6	7	8	9	10
• Personal Relationships	1	2	3	4	5	6	7	8	9	10
• Family/extended family	1	2	3	4	5	6	7	8	9	10
• Friends/social life	1	2	3	4	5	6	7	8	9	10
• Physical environment	1	2	3	4	5	6	7	8	9	10
• Fun and Recreation	1	2	3	4	5	6	7	8	9	10

Low Mood   High Mood

• How would you describe your emotional state? _____

Remember to review your scores on a regular basis.

21

Once you have completed this process it might be an idea to write down some of the problems you are experiencing. At this time it is all right to make general statements such as;

"I'm not very fit."

"My diet is terrible."

"My finances are in a mess."

"My relationship is going badly."

"I'm unhappy with my job."

"I don't have many friends."

Later on we will come back to whatever 'problems' you have identified and then work through a process that will help you deal with them more effectively.

It is very important to remember this is not about "beating yourself up" it's about helping you to get an idea of areas you might want to do some work on.

If, after a few weeks of completing the survey, your scores are consistently low in one area this might well indicate that you need to address this area and do something to meet the need that has not been met.

With regards to your emotional state. If you remain in a low or high mood high for a long period of time then you need to do something to change your mood as this may be a warning sign that you are particularly stressed at this time.

In the 'resources' section of this book you will find a "Life Situation Log Sheet" which will allow you to keep a record of your scores on a regular basis.

Learning How To Relax

"When the mind is overwhelmed, all words fail."

Proverb

Learning how to relax is placed at the forefront of this book because it is considered to be one of the most important skills to learn in living more effectively or when making any changes in your life. It is, in my view and the view of many others, essential for anyone in the process of making any changes in their life that they understand the relaxation response in order for the change process to be effective. This is because life and all forms of change will usually involve some level of emotional arousal such as frustration, anger, anxiety or stress. So, once you've decided to make changes in your life you need to be able to remain calm before you can learn how to do things differently.

I cannot stress too strongly how important the ability to relax is and how important it is when you or anyone else decides to make any changes in life. Many books may talk a little about relaxation but few of them emphasise how important the ability to relax is.

(More information on how important the relaxation response is and its effects on the sympathetic and parasympathetic nervous system is available in the Additional Resources Section.)

Here are some of the key points that you need to know:

• When relaxed you can't be anxious because you cannot experience two opposing states at the same time. This is because any strong emotion locks you into a single viewpoint and the "thinking part of the brain" simply cannot function properly, which is why you can often appear stupid when you are emotionally aroused - the higher learning centres of the brain simply cannot work when hijacked by emotion. Relaxation helps unlock the emotionally driven state allowing the "thinking part of the brain" to work more effectively and help you to consider or experience other viewpoints and solutions to difficulties.

• All **real learning** usually takes place in the relaxed state: that's when the ability to see things from multiple viewpoints ocurs and, consequently, generate creative insights. This illustrates the difference between conditioning and learning. You can be *conditioned* with new behaviour or beliefs when you are emotionally aroused but you cannot *understand* and really learn in a high state of emotional arousal. People can appear to enjoy being conditioned (by cults, emotionally arousing therapy etc.) but essentially what is happening is that their will and ability to choose is taken away and they are exploited. We need to ask ourselves if it is right to exploit people in this way.

There are many ways to achieve a relaxed state. I am going to concentrate on relaxation techniques that can be used by anyone.

Diaphragmatic breathing *(also known as the 7/11 technique)*

This is a simple but powerful technique that is easy to learn. It has an immediate beneficial effect and can be used as an exercise. It takes the following form:

1. Inhale to a count of seven.

2. Exhale to a count of eleven.

The reason for making the out-breath last longer is that inhalation has been shown to trigger the sympathetic nervous system (arousal) and exhalation stimulates the parasympathetic nervous system (the relaxation response). By breathing out more slowly than breathing in, you strengthen the relaxation response over the arousal response.

Muscle tension/relaxation

This ancient Yoga technique is also very effective. Ask the client if they would like to learn it and, if they do, talk them through the following routine. It's best if they can sit in a comfortable chair.

"Tense your feet" (pause for a count of ten) *...relax your feet."*

"Tense your calf muscles, (pause for a count of ten) *...relax your calf muscles.".*

"Tense your knees, (pause for a count of ten) *...relax your knees. "Tense your thigh muscles,* (pause for a count of ten) *...relax your thigh muscles. "*

"Tense your tummy muscles, (pause for a count of ten) *...relax your tummy."*

...and so on covering neck and shoulders, face muscles, arms and hands. This, as you will notice, not only relaxes them but focuses their attention on their body in the here and now.

At this point you might like to think of relaxation methods that you have used and then practise them.

Using a 'counting down' relaxation induction

Relaxation gives you immediate evidence that things can be different and enables you to think more clearly (because the emotional arousal has been reduced).

The counting down induction, sometimes called the 'staircase' induction, is appropriate for use with relaxation, visualisation and metaphor work.

It works with almost everybody because it mirrors what happens when we begin to drift off to sleep - the analytical part of our brain switches off and the other side of the brain summons up imagery.

(If you would like a CD of the counting down relaxation technique and other guided imagery sessions then one is available by contacting Ross Brittleton at **info@elementals.net**).

Different people have different ways of relaxing and it is very important to find a method that works for you. Other examples of relaxation can be found in the Resources Section.

Other well known ways of stimulating the relaxation response are activities such as *Meditation, Mindfulness practice, Feldenkrais work, Alexander classes, Yoga* and *T'ai Chi*.

All of the above activities have one thing in common and that is they stimulate the relaxation response. Remember, the key idea with relaxation skills is that you are **focusing** your **attention** (creating a trance state) in a way that relaxes you.

Emotions

"Even the most impersonal decisions are dictated by our emotions, it is only a question of degree."

M Feldenkrais

The ability to recognise and manage your emotions is another key element in living effectively, managing change, developing self-awareness, and expressing yourself. It is important to remember that emotions are natural and it is **how** you react in a specific situation that is most important.

In order to understand and manage your emotions well you first have to be able to identify them and be aware of their influence in your life. To help you do this look at the chart below. There are eight basic emotional states identified and then in each column below varying degrees of each emotion.

Read the chart below and become familiar with it so that in the future you can become aware of which emotions are triggered when you begin to change things in your life.

Anger	**Sadness**	**Enjoyment**	**Fear**
Irritation	Unhappiness	Pleasure	Anxiety
Annoyance	Disappointment	Happiness	Worry
Fury	Despondency	Joy	Concern
Outrage	Hurt	Delight	Embarrassment
Resentment	Grief	Effervescence	Defeat
Exasperation	Loneliness	Comfort	Remorse
Indignation	Despair	Exhilaration	Humiliation
Animosity	Depression	Excitement	Mortification
Hostility	Dejection	Contentment	Envy
Violence	Self-pity	Relief	
Protectiveness	Gloom	Pride	
Rage		Thrill	
Disgust	**Surprise**	**Love**	**Shame**
Contempt	Shock	Acceptance	Guilt
Disdain	Astonishment	Respect	Frustration
Scorn	Amazement	Friendliness	Embarrassment
Distaste	Wonder	Trust	Defeat
Revulsion	Awe	Kindness	Remorse
Aversion		Devotion	Humiliation

If there are some emotions that have not been mentioned then add them to your list.

Once you've looked at the chart and taken the time to identify the emotions that are most dominant in your life you can now write them on the chart below. For example if **'anger'** is present frequently and is also strong it will appear in the top right hand area of the chart. This will give you an instant indicator to the frequency this emotion occurs in your life and its strength. You can then decide if you need to take action to manage this emotion more effectively.

Charting The Frequency of Emotions

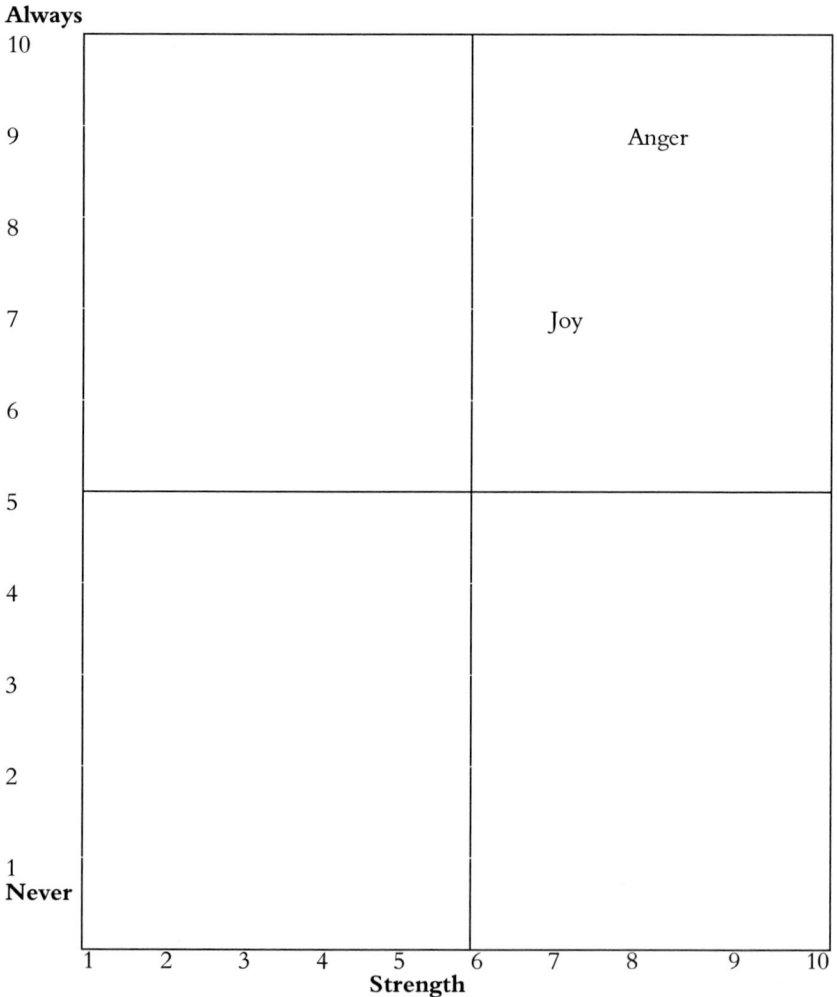

Always

```
10 |                    |                         |
   |                    |                         |
 9 |                    |         Anger           |
   |                    |                         |
 8 |                    |                         |
   |                    |                         |
 7 |                    |         Joy             |
   |                    |                         |
 6 |                    |                         |
   |---------------------------------------------|
 5 |                    |                         |
   |                    |                         |
 4 |                    |                         |
   |                    |                         |
 3 |                    |                         |
   |                    |                         |
 2 |                    |                         |
   |                    |                         |
 1 |                    |                         |
```
Never

```
    1    2    3    4    5    6    7    8    9    10
                    Strength
```

Habits for Responding to Feelings[1]
The Snake

Once upon a time there was a fierce and venomous snake. One day this snake met a sage and, overpowered by the sage's gentleness, lost its ferocity. The sage advised it to stop hurting people, and the snake resolved to live a life of innocence, without harming anyone.

But as soon as the people in a nearby village realised that the snake wasn't dangerous anymore, they started to throw stones at it, to drag it by the tail and tease it in innumerable ways. The snake was having a very hard time.

Luckily, the sage passed by the place again, and after seeing how badly battered the snake was and listening to its complaints, he simply said:

"My friend, I told you to stop hurting people - I didn't tell you never to hiss at them and scare them away. There is no harm in hissing at wicked men and at your enemies, showing that you can protect yourself and know how to resist evil. Only you must be careful not to pour your venom into the blood of your enemy. Resist not evil by causing evil in return".

Having identified the most dominant emotions in your life you can now deepen your understanding of these emotions and the effects they have on your life.

We are creatures of habit and as a result of this can lose awareness of what we are doing and how we respond. If you have decided to change then you may well have to have to break some of your habits and put new behaviours in their place. For many people this can be hard and when things get difficult they may well slip back into their old habits. This is part of the process of change and if you remember this you will see 'setbacks' as feedback on your strategy and then make changes to your approach because *"we forget first what we learnt last!"*

To change your habits you need to become aware of them and the following exercise can help you get a handle on some of your beliefs about the nature of anger/sadness/happiness/fear. It is on these beliefs that your habits are based. Read the following items in a state of relaxed concentration, and allow yourself to honestly fill in the blanks with your reactions. If you need more space, use some notepaper

1.   A time when I really felt _____ at another human being was:

(insert emotion)

2.   At that time I chose to :

3.   As I remember that experience now I feel :

4.   If I had allowed my _____ to be reflected in my body and in my voice in a manner that was absolutely uncensored, I imagine that I would have:

5.   The _____ that I ever recall seeing anybody be was:

6.   When I witnessed him or her being that _____, I felt:

7.   When my mother was _____, she tended to:

8.   When my father was _____, he tended to

9.   It seems to me that I automatically associate _____ with (choose all that apply):

a.	Power	f.	Pain
b.	Good	g.	Aliveness
c.	Bad	h.	Excitement
d.	Productivity	i.	Darkness
e.	Masculinity	j.	Creativity
		k.	Harm

Add your own responses:
l.
m

There is no need for you to be frightened or cautious about acknowledging your emotions, beliefs or habits. Doing so does not necessarily imply that you need to change anything. The key thing to do is to think through the validity of these emotions, beliefs or habits for you at this stage of your life, remembering that a habitual, emotional response, which made sense when it was formed, may have little value in your life as you currently experience it.

As you are now in a position to recognise and understand your emotions more effectively you might want to think a little about how you can now 'manage' your emotions so that they serve you and not you serve them. Earlier the 'relaxation response' was discussed and several methods of relaxation were described. You can use any or all of these methods in 'managing' your emotions and, as a reminder, some of these are listed below:

- Counting slowly to 10 before you respond.
- 7:11 Breathing
- Progressive Muscle relaxation
- Guided Imagery session
- Exercise
- Listening to relaxing music
- Doing a visualisation session as described later in the book and also available on CD by writing to: **info@elementals.net**
- T'ai Chi
- Yoga

I would urge you very strongly to choose one or more of the methods outlined above and to incorporate them into your life. Best results will be obtained if you do your chosen method on a regular basis. A little every day is considered far better than doing some relaxation once or twice a week.

You might want to repeat the same exercise with other emotions such as sadness, fear and joy or any others listed above. A copy of this exercise can be found in the Resources Section.

As you make your way through this book and learn about values, beliefs, metaphors and boundaries your understanding and awareness of what triggers emotional reactions will increase and your *'emotional intelligence'* will develop.

The Art of Living

Values

"When we align our thoughts, emotions and actions with the highest part of ourselves, we are filled with enthusiasm, purpose and meaning."

Gary Zukav

Yapko[1], *Egan*[2] and *Collins*[3] all believe that there is one key aspect of who you are that is more significant than the others: your values. In fact, most of your other behaviours are directly related to your value system. I would like to focus on your values as they relate to making changes in your life. Then we can take a closer look at each of the patterns that most influence how you live and your experience of life.

Most experts agree that it is in your first twenty years that the largest part of your entire personal value system is developed and integrated.

What is a value system? Your value system is a mostly unconscious but strongly internalised framework for forming judgments about, and reactions to, the events of your life. Through your value system, whether you realise it or not, you make judgements about each and every experience you have, evaluating what is normal and not normal, good and bad, right and wrong,

In order to help you identify the strongest values in your life look at the list on the next page and choose the 10 values and behaviours that most represent who you are and not what you desire to become? Once you have decided on your top 10 values keep a copy of the list as you will be asked to use it again later.

1.	achievement	39.	honesty
2.	adaptability	40.	human rights
3.	balance (home/work)	41.	humility
4.	balance (physical/mental/ emotional/ spiritual)	42.	humour/fun
		43.	image
5.	being liked	44.	independence
6.	being the best	45.	initiative
7.	caution	46.	innovation
8.	clarity	47.	integrity
9.	commitment	48.	interdependence
10.	community service	49.	job security
11.	compassion	50.	knowledge
12.	compromise	51.	listening
13.	conflict resolution	52.	logic
14.	conformity	53.	making a difference
15.	continuous learning	54.	mission focus
16.	control	55.	open communication
17.	cooperation	56.	openness
18.	counselling	57.	performance
19.	creativity	58.	perseverance
20.	dialogue	59.	personal fulfilment
21.	diversity	60.	personal growth
22.	ease with uncertainty	61.	power
23.	education	62.	pride
24.	efficiency	63.	professional growth
25.	empathy	64.	quality
26.	enthusiasm	65.	reliability
27.	environmental awareness	66.	respect
28.	ethics	67.	responsibility
29.	excellence	68.	reward
30.	experience	69.	risk-taking
31.	fairness	70.	safety
32.	family	71.	security
33.	financial stability	72.	self-discipline
34.	forgiveness	73.	success
35.	friendship	74.	tradition
36.	future generations	75.	trust
37.	generosity	76.	vision
38.	health	77.	wealth
		78.	wisdom

Societal Values[4]

There are certain values that are dominant in our society and have a strong influence on us all. Some of these are presented in the table below. The next exercise is to score these values.

This exercise will help you recognise how much you are influenced by these values and help you to learn how each of them can influence the quality of your life through the choices you make.

Use a scoring system from 1 to 10 (10 being very important) that reflects how important each value is to you.

VALUE	Low									High
Achievement	1	2	3	4	5	6	7	8	9	10
Being	1	2	3	4	5	6	7	8	9	10
Emotionally Contained	1	2	3	4	5	6	7	8	9	10
Emotionally Expressive	1	2	3	4	5	6	7	8	9	10
Logical	1	2	3	4	5	6	7	8	9	10
Emotional	1	2	3	4	5	6	7	8	9	10
Materialistic	1	2	3	4	5	6	7	8	9	10
Spiritual	1	2	3	4	5	6	7	8	9	10
Task Focused	1	2	3	4	5	6	7	8	9	10
People Focused	1	2	3	4	5	6	7	8	9	10
Isolated	1	2	3	4	5	6	7	8	9	10
Connected	1	2	3	4	5	6	7	8	9	10
Self Oriented	1	2	3	4	5	6	7	8	9	10
Other Oriented	1	2	3	4	5	6	7	8	9	10
Conformist	1	2	3	4	5	6	7	8	9	10
Individualistic	1	2	3	4	5	6	7	8	9	10
Competition	1	2	3	4	5	6	7	8	9	10
Co-operation	1	2	3	4	5	6	7	8	9	10
Tradition	1	2	3	4	5	6	7	8	9	10
Change	1	2	3	4	5	6	7	8	9	10
Security	1	2	3	4	5	6	7	8	9	10
Risk	1	2	3	4	5	6	7	8	9	10
Depth	1	2	3	4	5	6	7	8	9	10
Variety	1	2	3	4	5	6	7	8	9	10

Opposing Values

All of us *must* make judgments about our experiences in order to have a meaningful way of relating to them. For example, we each make judgments about other people because such judgments give us an organized way, *even if it's an incorrect one,* for responding to them. In short, making judgments is necessary in order to create a plan of action. On the basis of your value system, you are more likely to seek out one type of desirable experience, thereby excluding another type of experience. You develop certain capabilities that seem important or worthwhile, and you ignore others that you view as less necessary or valuable. You can't be everywhere learning everything! If, for example, you were learning how to cope with a difficult family environment, then you weren't learning how to relax and enjoy easy, comfortable relationships. This is a simple but significant concept, particularly in viewing change and development as often arising from incomplete or incorrect learnings. *The things you don't know how to do can cause you problems.*

It may be useful to think of a value as existing on different ends of a scale, as shown in the table below, with opposites found at the extremes and with lots of space between to represent different views about that value. I could describe many values that an individual may hold. Some are more powerful than others, though, in affecting your outlook and responses.

Achievement	v	Simply 'Being'
Emotional Expressiveness	v	Emotional Containment
Being More Emotional	v	Being More Logical
Materialism	v	Spirituality
Being Connected To Others	v	Being Isolated
Being Other Orientated	v	Being Self-Orientated
Being Task-Orientated	v	Being People Orientated
Being A Conformist	v	Being An Individualist
Being Competitive	v	Being Co-Operative
Maintaining Tradition	v	Making Changes
Taking Risks	v	Being Safe
Seeking Depth	v	Seeking Variety in Experience

As you look at the 'opposing values' above, take some time to consider how each of the values is relevant to you personally. Think about the values you hold and how deeply you hold them. Consider, for example, the sixth pair of 'opposites', *"other-oriented"* on one side and *"self-oriented"* the other. No one is completely other-oriented, nor is anyone entirely self-oriented. However, an individual's personal experience can lead him to be too intensely one or the other. Such an imbalance can create problems when you are in the process of change.

For instance, consider the value system of women. Despite the gains in equal opportunities for women, many women still learn a value system that emphasises being *"other-oriented"*. Mothers frequently advise their daughters to be good wives, good mothers, and good daughters. Such value-laden advice essentially says, *"your worth comes from what you do in relation to other people, not from who you are as an individual."* This value is very different from one that says, *"create and pursue your own independent dreams; they are as, or more, important than marrying or having children"*.

Relate this value to, *"conformity"* and *"individuality."* If a woman is taught to be a good wife and a good mother, to meet those expectations successfully she would have to conform to the demands of roles that she did not create, ones that may not fit her very well. After all, let's be realistic: not everyone is good spouse or parent material. To suppress or override dimensions of yourself in order to obtain approval from others places your self-esteem in their hands. It is difficult, if not impossible, to develop truly healthy self-esteem under such circumstances.

Considering the role that values play in processing all of your life experiences, it is easy to see how they create patterns of behaviour that put you at risk for a variety of difficulties when contemplating change. For example, based on what we know about the value that says, *"be other-oriented and conform to the expectations and demands of others"* in traditional female roles, is it any wonder that women find it very difficult to change? How can you find change easy when too much of your self-esteem rests on other people's reactions to you? The opposing values of *"other-orientation"* and the *"need to conform"* highlight how the values you are taught can lead you to seek out life experiences that may ultimately work against your well-being.

Each of the values listed above is neutral. In itself it is neither positive or negative. Rather, each derives its value only in relation to the many aspects of your life. Consider, for example, how a typical man in this culture learns to be achievement-oriented, having been taught from an early age that his worth is determined by his accomplishments. It should be no surprise, then, when he has high professional expectations and works hard to achieve them, putting even his relationships with his wife and family second to his work. And as long as circumstances permit him to express his need to achieve, his value of achievement can earn him great rewards in the forms of approval from others, financial success, professional status, and so forth. If, on the other hand, circumstances change, he may face a crisis. If this man is unable to continue achieving, for whatever reason, then the central focus of his life is lost, and problems inevitably follow. The significant point here is this:

Values can create rigid patterns of behaviour that put any changes you are making at risk if those values are challenged in some way.

Each of the values listed above can represent an entire way of life. Problems with change usually occur with the failure of the value system on which the person has based his life. You can predict the crisis proportions of a man's life when he has been forever climbing the career ladder, and suddenly his career is squashed by a layoff or a lengthy illness. And you can easily predict the probable outcome for a traditional female who completely builds her life around others (her husband, her children), who then leave her. If such individuals are able to deal effectively with the situation at hand, adjusting in a timely manner to the changes forced on them, they are much less likely to experience problems.

How Strong Are Your Values Part II?[4]

Go through each of the top 10 personal values you chose earlier and the values listed in the 'Opposing Values table' which you also gave scores to. Check that you have given each of them a score on a scale ranging from 1 to 10, that reflects how strongly (10) or how weakly (1), you believe, you hold that value. How do you know? Using the table below, or a blank piece of paper, specify the behaviours you engage in that reflect the value. The more extreme your numbers, the more easily you can identify which values represent your greatest potential strengths and greatest weaknesses. Use the outline below to help organise your thoughts.

Value	Its Relative Strength	Behaviours that Reflect that Value

Personal Wishes in the Real World

The emphasis on values in this section is meant to highlight how finely balanced your awareness of your values must be with the actions that you take in life. Consider your internal experience when you respond to a feeling or a situation in terms of how you think you "should" feel or what you think you "should" value when, in reality, you don't feel that way. Being clear about what your values are and living according to those values but also balancing your internal beliefs and wishes against external realities are very important aspects of feeling good.

Patterns of Change

Well before the effects of setbacks occur, the risk factors are usually in place. Too often, people notice, or respond to, the most obvious triggering event and never see the invisible risk factors (such as their values, their emotional state or their physical health) that made them vulnerable in the first place. This point has tremendous preventive value. It is imperative, therefore, to examine your values in order to determine the strengths each permits you, as well as any associated limitations that may put you at risk later.

In order to make lasting changes in your life and live life well, you really need to acknowledge your values and seek to maintain a lifestyle that reflects them consistently. Sometimes, failure and disappointment arises from situations where we disappoint ourselves by saying or doing something that violates our own values or how we think we "should" be. To feel good, it is also important to acknowledge the value of experiences that lie outside the boundaries of your previous experiences. Learning to do so is how you can actively develop a greater degree of flexibility. Maintaining balance in your life means being able to change effectively with the changing times, comfortably adjusting to circumstances as the need dictates.

Also remember that the values you learned early in your life may have little to do with living life well today. For example, assuming that once you marry someone, he or she will always be there for you is an older, albeit better, concept of marriage, but one that doesn't hold up so well today in light of divorce statistics. You can't assume someone will always be there. Rather, you will have to find someone who shares the values and skills that help make an enduring marriage possible.

Do your values fit with current realities? I'm a firm believer that when what you're doing doesn't work, you have to adjust to the reality of the circumstances and do something else! So take this opportunity to discover what your values are, how they influence your life and how you can use them when you are making changes in your life.

(If you would like to discover which values are most dominant in your life then you may well find it of interest to complete the Values in Action Questi (VIA Survey), devised by Dr Martin Seligman, a psychologist and author or "Authentic Happiness". The questionnaire is available, free, on **www.authentichappiness.org**. *Try it. I'm sure you'll be interested in the results.)*

Boundaries[1]

Another important factor in living effectively is understanding how important it is to be aware of your personal boundaries. We will look at defining your boundaries and then look at building and protecting *your* boundaries.

Your boundaries define who you are, what social role you are in at the moment, what you can and cannot do while you are in that role, what you will and will not accept in others' treatment of you, and which part(s) of yourself you will engage with at the moment.

Without clear, firm boundaries, you are at a constant risk of being taken advantage of by others or yourself and the process of change sabotaged.

Defining Your Roles and Boundaries

How many roles do you currently occupy in your life? Consider some of the possibilities. Parent? Child? Employer? Employee? Friend? Colleague? Citizen? Group member? These terms all represent roles you assume at different times in your life. Having a clear understanding of your roles will help you in any changes you are making.

To help you identify your own roles in life use the list opposite and mark the ones that apply to you,

Each role has specific demands that define success when you meet them or failure when you don't. It takes personal strength and integrity to maintain those boundaries, especially when your feelings are pulling you in the direction of violating the boundaries. You must be able to go beyond those feelings and recognise that there is considerably more at stake than your feelings.

Why have boundaries? They define you as a person, they define what you do and don't do, and they define your relationships with others. They define your personal, social, and professional responsibilities and your level of integrity. If you think about it, much of the difficulty with change is because people ignore or reject the positive value of boundaries. Whenever people put their personal needs or desires ahead of their social responsibilities, the results can be harmful. Just because someone can, doesn't mean he should. When is ignoring boundaries a positive assertion of "personal freedom," and when is it irresponsible and self-indulgent? Finding the line and responding skillfully is not always easy.

Roles Summary

Individual Roles	Work Roles	Personal / Family Roles	Citizen Roles
Artist	Artist	Aunt	
Athlete	Associate	Brother	Advocate
Creator	Coach	Brother-in-law	Beautifier
Discoverer	Colleague	Cousin	Change Agent
Fool	Customer	Child / Teenager	Coach
Friend to Self	Doctor	Daughter	Community Activist
Hero/Heroine	Drone	Father	Council Member
Hunter	Entrepreneur	Father-in-law	Crime Fighter
Leader	Lawyer	Friend	Elder
Learner	Leader	Mother	Letter Writer
Magician	Mover & Shaker	Mother-in-law	Nature lover
Meditator	Pawn	Nephew	Neighbour
Sage	Service Provider	Niece	Office Holder
Saint	Student	Sister	Organizer
Warrior	Subordinate	Son	Philanthropist
	Supervisor	Stepfather	Revolutionary
	Teacher	Stepmother	Volunteer
	Visionary	Uncle	Voter
	Wage slave		
	Worker		
	Writer		

What are *your* boundaries? They are usually clear in the interactions between you and others and in your interactions with yourself. Throughout your life, you have had countless opportunities to discover your boundaries by learning what you like and what you don't like, what you do and don't feel comfortable with, what is and is not acceptable to you, and what you are and are not willing to say or do to others or yourself.

Developing Boundaries

How do we learn and then develop our boundaries? Throughout our childhood we are taught, by others, how to treat people, how to treat ourselves, and how to respond to the demands and expectations of others. Through all these interactions, we learn whether we are acceptable just for being who we are, or whether our worth comes from how much of ourselves we sacrifice to gain the approval or love of others. Boundaries are easiest to build when you are encouraged to know and express yourself as an individual, and your uniqueness is valued. That is not the same, though, as "anything goes." Ideally, you are taught to honour and accept yourself, but not by acting irresponsibly at others' expense.

Consider a simple example that involves parents, children, and boundaries. When you were growing up, did you have privacy as a member of your family? Did you have your own "personal space"? This is not referring to your own bedroom, but to your space for doing routine things. Could you speak privately on the telephone to friends, or did your parents insist on listening in? Were you left alone to talk and play with your friends? If you were taking a bath or shower, did people respect your privacy, or did they intrude? Did you have a private place for your things, or did anything you have quickly become a matter of public knowledge? Did people talk openly about aspects of you that should have been private, like your body or your deeper feelings about sensitive issues?

You may think of specific instances where your boundaries were ignored, such as when someone revealed a secret. However such exceptional situations do not usually create poor personal boundaries. Rather, boundary problems develop from growing up under *continuing* violations, in which a sense of the importance of self is not allowed to develop. In such cases, people's boundaries either never develop, or they are torn down and ignored again and again. The results can be devastating on many levels, as you can imagine. Such hurtful experiences define you as powerless to protect yourself against deeply personal intrusions. There is rarely anything empowering about such painful experiences; usually they are only destructive, requiring a great deal of effort just to cope with them.

Without boundaries people will take advantage of you, there may be victimisation, helplessness, self-loathing, and negativity. It is essential, then, to learn that, though your boundaries may have been non-existent or indefensible in the past, in your process of change the boundaries can be built and protected and become a source of pride and self-value".

Managing Role Conflicts

The first part of the process of defining your boundaries was to become aware of the various roles that you play in life. Now you can define your boundaries in terms of the relationship between your boundaries and your behaviour. Before going any further do the exercise below called "Managing Role Conflicts". In this exercise, you are asked to prepare for inevitable role conflicts.

This exercise will help you define the many roles you fill and how to decide which one to respond to in a given situation when two or more roles are in conflict.[2]

Even when everything is going well, it's hard to meet all of life's demands as parent, child, employee, citizen and more. When your obligations conflict, you need to make tough choices. Using the list of roles you marked earlier use the table below to become aware of the expectations associated with each role?

Roles I play	Behaviours associated with this role	Behaviours not allowed by that role	In case of this role conflicting with another, I can... (fill in the blank)

Now you are more able to think in terms of boundaries and how they might affect you when you are making changes in your life, you can also notice the effects of change in your life when you live up to the behaviours listed in column two, or when you do any of the behaviours in column three.

The King Who Sought Personal Empowerment

Once a king commanded his advisors to tell him something that would empower him, help him overcome obstacles in his life, help him to achieve goals, and energise him to move forward. The advisors told him everything they knew, but he rejected it all, saying he had heard it all before. "Yes, yes," said the king, "you've told me all these things already. Tell me something new that will really empower me."

Finally, the advisors told him about an old wise man who lived in a cave on top of a mountain on the other side of the world who knew everything and could answer his question. The advisors cautioned the king that the journey to see the man was long, tiresome, and dangerous. One had to travel across stormy, turbulent oceans, cross burning deserts, tramp through snake-infested jungles, cross rivers with piranhas and other man-eating creatures, and finally climb a high mountain that even guides refused to climb.

The king insisted that he still must go despite the advisor's protestations. So he went on the voyage, travelled the oceans, crossed the deserts, tramped the jungles and rivers, and climbed the mountain till he found the cave.

Inside, the king saw an old man with a white beard, wearing only a loincloth, staring into the fire. The king began to talk to the old man, but he stopped the king, telling him he already knew why he was here and would soon answer the question.

After a long period of silence, the old man looked at the king and said, "If your want to achieve your goals, overcome obstacles, empower yourself and move forward in your life, look no further than the breath in your own body. Everyday in the morning, every night and several times during the day, you must say this:"

"If it's to be, it's up to me. If it's to be, it's up to me."

Metaphor

All of us use our imaginations to describe things and link the description to an object or action. The connection is not real it a descriptive term. For example when we say *"you can cut the atmosphere with a knife."* In this example you know that you cannot really use a knife to cut the atmosphere it is merely a way you have chosen to describe a particular situation. Among other things the brain is a metaphorical instrument and metaphorical patterns have to be completed in the outside environment in order to allow flexibility of response. To make effective changes it is vital to understand what this means.

Metaphor is part of everyday language and experience, even for the simplest things. It is through metaphor that we communicate because the naked truth cannot be spoken. The nearest we can get to truth is by clothing it in metaphor. Thus we are forced by the nature of things to describe anything at all by beginning, *"It's like..."* or using phrases like *"He's a rock!"*, *"Quick as a flash!"*, *"A bolt out of the blue."* This is so from the simplest examples, such as describing a new taste experience, right up to more complex things.

When people are dealing well with life's ups and downs and changes they are drawing on appropriate metaphors to steer their way through. For example they may say *"a problem shared is a problem halved"* or *'life's a bowl of cherries'* or *"every cloud has a silver lining."* As a result they tend to manage any problems they encounter more effectively. However when people develop problems or encounter difficulties with change they are probably drawing on inappropriate metaphors. They may say to themselves and others things like: *"I'm a glass half-empty type of person"* or *"it never rains but it pours"* or *"life's an uphill struggle!"* They are distorting their current reality by using what they have learned in the past in a different, unrelated situation (albeit beguilingly similar) to make sense of it. So a young woman may bring her earlier experience of a failed relationship into a new relationship with a loving partner, reacting with distrust and fear and a need to stay in control. Now, when those 'metaphorical templates' are appropriate to our situation, there is no problem - they work beautifully. The map, so to speak, is accurate. But when the emotional templates do not match sufficiently well with our present reality, we have a problem.

47

The recognition that we may have an inaccurate map of reality, and that we can develop a more accurate one, gives enormous scope to people when making changes in their lives.

When people understand the faulty templates they developed in their attempt to structure their lives to survive the inadequacies of their environmental and learning experiences, it becomes easier for them to detach from them and move on. But they can only review and understand their past in this way if, first, they learn to become less emotional about it.

In other words you need to develop a dispassionate understanding of your own past and create a new future.

Memory is both a constructive and creative experience. When we access a memory in the present, to illustrate a point or solve a problem, we do so through metaphor. Our brain automatically goes on a metaphorical search, looking for experiences in the past that will confirm our idea of what we think our problem is about.

This means that anyone thinking about their past experiences is inevitably going to come up with metaphorical representations of their current predicament. So, you can often hear expressions like *'men are all the same'* or *'it's like wading through mud'* or *'my glass is half empty.'* This, however, doesn't necessarily mean that the metaphorical representations are true: it is simply a reflection of how the problem is understood in the person's mind. Memory has to distort the past in order to get the best metaphorical fit to the idea that's prompting the search. Neither does it follow that those 'metaphorical' comparisons of a current dilemma are in fact the origin of that dilemma. Because a memory is largely recreated each time it is recalled, we cannot be sure that the comparative pattern it comes up with is a significant contributor to the presenting problem. Once you recognise that a 'metaphorical template' may well be wrong, it really doesn't matter at what point it is changed, or what specific instance of its existence is changed, so long as the pattern is altered.

Change through metaphor

The very metaphorical process that creates problems when things don't go as planned can also be used to help manage change more effectively. So, for instance, if you have a habit behaving like a *'bull in a china shop'* or *'jumping in with both feet'* you could choose another metaphor and consider the expression *'look before you leap,'* or *'discretion is the better part of valour'* or think about the story of the *'tortoise and the hare.'*

Just using that metaphor can help you consider a different approach to take and thus adapt your approach to change.

Metaphors and stories – Once upon a time...

There are several reasons you can make use of metaphors and stories and these include:

1) Building a sense of expectancy

If you can create a sense of expectancy then you create in yourself the idea that change is possible and can be achieved.

2) Bypass natural resistance to change.

Stories often make you aware of possibilities. People often have rigid views about life that prevent them from changing. Stories can often bypass this rigidity and help you form a new perspective on the challenges you face. By reading different 'stories' you can become aware of different possibilities and there is less pressure to consider the options.

3) Create independence.

When presented with a story you usually have to make sense of the meaning of the story and decide for yourself whether to take action based on this new perspective. The process also increases flexibility of thinking, since understanding metaphor requires the right side of the brain, which is more involved in imagery.

4) Help you to recognise yourself.

A story can help you see yourself as you are in reality.

Here's a story for you to read and think about what it means to you:

The Wind And The Sun

The North Wind and the Sun once had a dispute as to which of them was the stronger. They both recounted their achievements but still the matter was left unsettled. They agreed to settle the dispute once and for always by having a contest, As just then a traveller came into view, they decided the winner would be the one who could make the traveller take off his coat the soonest.

The boastful North Wind was the first to try, while the Sun watched from behind a grey cloud, The North Wind blew a fierce blast and nearly tore the man's coat open,' but the man responded by pulling his coat even more tightly around himself The more fiercely the North Wind blasted him, the more determinedly the man held on to his coat. Finally, the North Wind gave up in despair and said to the Sun,

"You won't be able to do any better".

Then out came the kindly Sun, sending down his warmest rays upon the traveller's head. The man looked up gratefully at the Sun but soon felt faint with the heat. He took off his coat and hastened to the trees for comfort in the nearest shade.

One possible interpretation could be that The North Wind represents people who see themselves as superior to others, the possessor of wisdom, which gives them the authority to instruct others on how to handle their lives,

Unfortunately such an approach usually provokes resistance in a person who will then ignore the proffered advice, just as the man in the fable pulled the coat more tightly around him in response to the direct, confrontational approach of the North Wind,

The more indirect approach of the Sun had a very different effect on the man's behaviour. The warmth created by the Sun's initial approach is analogous to rapport building, The Sun starts out by evoking a warm, pleasant feeling in the person whose behaviour it wants to change. The man in the story becomes warmer still and *he perceives* that he no longer needs the protection of the coat and so he takes it off. This is like a person discarding things in their life that are no longer useful.

The man, having taken off his coat, next heads to the trees for shelter. This can be seen as the person finding his or her own solution to their problem. Just as the warmth of the Sun prompted the man to see the need to do something different, so the suggestions in our metaphors can prompt you to see the need to change your life or behaviour.

The telling of stories like this is common to all cultures and tends to evoke pleasant, non-threatening associations in the listener as it is often associated with childhood or time spent relaxing with friends. Storytelling has been used to entertain, pass on cultural values and to instruct people for many thousands of years.

Stories mean different things to different people and it's a good idea to expose yourself to many different types of stories as these will give you a rich variety of different choices you can make. Your unconscious, creative imagination will seek and find the 'meaning' that is relevant for your situation. No explanation, no direct statement of the story's meaning can substitute for the way it acts on the mind of the reader or hearer.

In the bibliography you will find a list of books that contain stories of all kinds, which you might find very useful. I recommend you take the time to read some of the stories in these books.

The Man Who Walked on Water

A conventionally minded dervish, from an austerely pious school, was walking one day along a river bank. He was absorbed in concentration on moralistic and scholastic problems, for this was the form which Sufi teaching had taken in the community to which he belonged. He equated emotional religion with the search for ultimate Truth.

*Suddenly his thoughts were interrupted by a loud shout: someone was repeating the dervish call. "There is no point in that," he said to himself, "because the man is mispronouncing the syllables. Instead of intoning **YA HU**, he is saying **U YA HU**".*

Then he realised that he had a duty, as a more careful student, to correct this unfortunate person, who might have no opportunity to be rightly guided, and was therefore probably only doing his best to attune himself to the idea behind the sounds.

So he hired a boat, and made his way to the island in midstream from which the sound appeared to come. There he found a man sitting in a reed hut, dressed in dervish robe, moving in time to his own repetition of the initiatory phrase. It is incumbent on me to tell you this, because there is merit for him who gives and for him who takes advice. This is the way in which you speak it," and he told him.

"Thank you" said the other dervish humbly.

The first dervish entered his boat again, full of satisfaction at having done a good deed. After all, it was said that a man who could repeat the sacred formula correctly could even walk on the water: something that he had never seen, but had always hoped - for some reason - to be able to achieve.

*Now he could hear nothing from the reed hut, but he was sure that his lesson had been well taken. Then he heard a faltering **U YA HU** as the second dervish started to repeat the phrase in his old way.*

While the first dervish was thinking about this, reflecting on the perversity of humanity and its persistence in error, he suddenly saw a strange sight. From the island, the other dervish was coming toward him, walking on the surface of the water.

Amazed, he stopped rowing. The second dervish walked up to him, and said, "Brother, I am sorry to trouble you, but I have come out to ask you again the standard method of making the repetition you were telling me, because I find it difficult to remember it."

Power Of Beliefs

As you go through life you carry with you a 'belief system' that helps you to make sense of the things that happen to you. Beliefs are 'assumptions' that you make that also influence what you do, say or think in your own mind as well as on a larger scale in relationships, organisations and government. 'Beliefs' are not facts, *'beliefs' use oversimplification to stop intelligent thought or analysis of words used.*

It is when you are very emotional that you oversimplify your thinking processes. To be effective you need to work in a way which makes sure that you don't let your own emotions become too aroused and thus reduce your own thought processes into tyrannical, black and white thinking. This is because strong emotions stop you connecting to reality.

Separating beliefs and opinions

As people we are in the process of living and change and we can often believe destructive and inefficient ideas and illogical ideas or myths. These will usually come across as unsubstantiated assertions and often delivered with emotion and a conviction that makes them sound as though they are proven facts.

Some of these myths derive from errors in perception, others from psychological errors due to emotional arousal, while still others are logical distortions.

Whatever their origins, these beliefs can take on a special life of their own when they are popularised in the media and become part of our national credo (such as faith in 'institutions', belief in astrology, appeals to the 'opinion of the majority'). Once they achieve this stature they hold a special attraction for those who seek the approval of others, 'experts' or authority figures by resorting to these commonly held misconceptions.

Illogical beliefs are most likely to creep into your inner dialogue when you are looking for evidence to counteract your unhelpful belief. You might, for example, say, *'Better safe than sorry?"* quoting a popular platitude without recognising that the platitude has nothing to do with the rules of evidence you are trying to get established if you are taking a cognitive approach, and therefore cannot be advanced as proof of an assertion.

One way to undermine what to you are your logical fallacies is to gradually become aware of them and become aware of how they are distorting your understanding of your situation. More often than not fallacies are held in place by high emotional arousal which stops you coming to grips with, and overturning, a lifetime's accumulation of mistaken perceptions.

Your job is to challenge and reframe those ideas so that these beliefs no longer have a negative influence on your life.

Challenging your belief system

To separate belief, assumptions and opinion from fact you first have to be aware of the beliefs, assumptions and opinions you have about yourself and your situation.

Here you have a collection of some typical beliefs. They are all illogical falsehoods. They are all forms of foolishness and common to normal people everywhere because they are fuelled by emotional arousal, anxiety, depression, greed, lust, vanity etc. - which we all exhibit at times.

You may recognise some of them operating in yourself.

1. *"It's dangerous to get nervous".*

2. *"I am inferior to Mike because he always beats me at squash".*

3. *"Anybody who can't spell is stupid".*

4. *"I'll never get over it".*

5. *"It's my (or my spouse's) fault that the marriage didn't last".*

6. *"All criminals are produced by bad parents".*

7. *"Anybody who is anxious all the time is really sick".*

8. *"I should never make mistakes".*

9. *"My husband is late; he must be having an affair".*

10. *Making 'wants' into 'musts,' 'oughts,' and 'shoulds'.*

11. *"I have to get her back".*

12. *"I'll never be happy if I don't get that house".*

13. *"I have a right to have what I want / be happy / be loved etc."*

14. *"I bumped into the table because I was trying to hurt myself."*

15. *"My sore shoulder must be caused by unconscious anxiety."*

16. *"He is basically lazy."*

17. *"Everybody should treat me nicely."*

18. *"I should get what I want in life."*

19. *"I am making my husband unhappy."*

20. *"He is going to have to get out of my way."*

21. *"When the going gets tough, the tough get going."*

22. *"If something can go wrong, it will."*

23. *"I'm not swimming. You can get diseases from sea water."*

24. *"You had to have been there to tell me what I did wrong."*

25. *"You have no qualifications, you can't know what you are talking about."*

26. *"I was traumatised in a past life".*

27. *"It's Fate."*

28. *"You're so stupid, ugly, and dumb. You don't know a thing!"*

29. *"How dare you criticise me! You have no damn right to do so."*

30. *"Everyone should know that ..."*

31. *"This problem is so complex we can never understand it."*

How to challenge harmful beliefs and false assumptions

When casting doubt on these unhelpful belief systems and emotional interpretations you need to remember the following seven principles:

1. Remain Calm

Make sure you are in a calm and relaxed state while challenging one of your beliefs. As mentioned earlier it is difficult to make good decisions if you are in a very emotional state.

2. Consider the evidence

Write a list of your most commonly held beliefs, opinions or assumptions on one side of a scale and solid evidence on the other, and the scale will instantly tip in favour of the evidence because logical fallacies are so flimsy when made concrete.

Once you recognise how essentially empty false assumptions are, you can learn to avoid resorting to these linguistic diversions. The best way to learn this is by finding examples and learning to counter every false assumption you utter, think or hear until you become fully aware of the pointlessness of these assertions. You can use some of the 'beliefs' listed above to help you in this process

3. Suspend judgement

If you have a firm belief about what is causing the problem then consider holding back these assumptions or judgements until such time that more information is available. Allow yourself to suspend judgement for a little while

4. Cast doubt on negative beliefs

We often assume that we are forced to behave in a certain way and that it is out of our control and this may be totally incorrect. If you hear yourself stating a negative belief you should look at it objectively and gently cast doubt on it. Play down negativity (and in some cases unrealistic positivity) in favour of a more neutral stance - *"Let's wait and see shall we?"*

Always be aware of over-positive beliefs whenever you feel that this attitude could potentially lead to failure because the expectations are too high.

5. Look for counter examples and anecdotes

Whenever you identify an example of an obstacle it is often useful to look for a counter example which neutralises it. Also you can ask friends about what they did in similar situations but found a different solution. Or, when you find a problem is impossible to overcome, you can ask others how they overcame the same problem.

6. Acknowledge and then ignore negative remarks

If you find yourself being continually negative just acknowledge the negative thought, focus on your breathing and then ignore it. In effect, you are simply choosing not to pick up on the negative remark. In the meantime continue to move in a positive direction.

7. Anticipate and then normalise the objections, complaints and exaggerated accounts

Learn to anticipate irrelevancies, black and white judgements, negative beliefs and remarks. By anticipating them you can prepare how you will deal with them in advance. By neutralising these negative comments you keep one step ahead and give yourself the chance of neutralising potential negativity. This is a skill that you can develop over time.

Examples of challenges

The interpretations that you give yourself can often be cut short by asking yourself a simple question. For example:

"Have I got evidence of that?"

"How do I know that?"

"She may say that but is she an expert in ...?"

Or by the following:

"Well, I could be right, or I could be wrong – I can't be sure."

"The opposite could be true."

"I'm sorry, I don't understand."

Optimist Or Pessimist?

Up until now we have discussed the influence of your emotions, your values, your beliefs and your needs on your ability to make changes in your life. As you've probably realised what you think and believe has an enormous impact on you and the way you live your life. There is one other part of the way you think that I'd like to discuss and this is known as your 'thinking style'. In short, whether you are an optimistic thinker or a pessimistic thinker: described in great detail by *Seligman* in his book *'Learned Optimism'¹*. In the process of change it is inevitable that you will experience setbacks and how you respond to these setbacks will, to a large part, be affected by whether your thinking style is optimistic or pessimistic.

The most important things affecting the way we think are:

- **How *personally* we take events**

  Do we tend to blame ourselves for *every* setback rather than considering all other possible reasons for something going wrong? If a relationship breaks down, for example, is it always our fault?

- **How *pervasive* we view events to be**

  If we lose a job do we think our whole life is ruined or do we limit the damage to a short period of time and see that now there is the possibility that other career opportunities can open up?

- **How *permanent* we think an event is**

  Whether we think a setback will be short lived or go on forever. If we don't get the house we have set our heart upon, for example, do we say, *"Oh well, perhaps something else even better will turn up,"* or *"I will never be happy again as long as I live?"*

If you take things personally, interpret events as all pervasive or all encompassing and think setbacks last forever, you are probably a 'pessimistic thinker' and likely to find change harder to cope with. This is because these emotionally driven black and white thinking styles inevitably generate more emotion by repeatedly turning on the fight or flight response which makes us angry (fight) or anxious (flight). In other words, when people imagine the worst the 'bad' things that can happen to them, magnifying them so that the whole of their life is affected, they are either making themselves feel very hostile (anger), or frightening themselves (anxiety).

This excessive turning on of the fight or flight response usually results in the *'all or nothing'* reaction to life events found in people with a *'pessimistic thinking style'* and explains why people who think like this find it difficult to break the whole down into relevant component parts. When thinking is heavily influenced by the emotional brain it cannot see the many shades of grey between different viewpoints. Many 'pessimistic thinkers' tend to be perfectionists. If an event they anticipated didn't go totally as planned, for example, for them it was a disaster; if a relationship isn't perfect, it is terrible.

Pessimistic thinkers will tend to make statements like:

"I'm useless."
"Why does this always happen to me."
"I'll never be able to change!"

Looking at the statements above you'll notice that they all express a personal (I/me), pervasive and permanent (always, never), point of view.

Optimists on the other hand generally think and talk in a completely different way. To them negative events are seen as temporary, not necessarily personal and relate to specific events. For example:

"I'm useless"
becomes
"I was useless at football last week."
"Why does this always happen to me?"
becomes
"Why was that man rude to me last night?"
"I'll never be able to change!"
becomes
"It may take me a little time but I'll do what I need to do to make the changes I want."

These statements may be **personal** but they have the common characteristics of being **temporary** and **specifically related to certain events**. As a result of this they are unlikely to have a long term effect on your mood or your emotional state or your attitude to change.

Most things that happen in life have many different causes. When we are more objective we can see the truth of this and we don't have to blame ourselves unreasonably when things go wrong. But 'pessimistic thinkers' are viewing the world in a negative way and therefore not seeing the options available. That is why they, so often, plump for the big, simple-minded, single cause to explain a setback. *"Either I am to blame or somebody else is to blame."* They either get unreasonably angry with someone else for their difficulties or see themselves as the cause of their difficulties, generating self-blame, low self-confidence and low self-esteem. *(If you would like to discover more about your 'thinking style' then complete "The Optimism Test", devised by Dr Martin Seligman, a psychologist and author or "Learned Optimism". The questionnaire is available, free, on www.authentichappiness.org).*

The Art of Living

Methods Of Motivation

The number of books and the theories on motivation are too numerous to mention. It is probably fair to say that the most dominant method of motivation used today is the 'carrot and stick' approach. This may well be the most widely used approach but Raj Persaud in his book *'The Motivated Mind'* makes the point that research has consistently shown that this method is, in fact, the least effective method to motivate people. Below I will outline various other methods of motivation that have, in the long term, been shown to be more effective and will also give you a wider range of approaches you can adopt both in motivating yourself and others.

1. The utilisation principle

At the heart of living effectively is the fundamental principle of using what 'tools' you already have as a natural way of facilitating solutions. In other words, your interests, habits, way of speaking etc. may all contain skills and strategies that can be used to help. Everyone is unique and has unique talents and you may well be able to use these to bring about change in your life. This includes both conscious and unconscious offerings, resources, strengths, experiences, abilities (or disabilities), relationships, attitudes, problems, symptoms, deficits, environment, vocations, hobbies, aversions, values, emotions. ..the list is endless, but the concept is simple. If it's part of your life, it may have a use in achieving a goal *and* if you already have it then you don't need to introduce something new.

When you've tried a strategy and it's failed you may have to take a step back and review your strategy. For example, if you have a great sense of what is 'right' and what is 'wrong' then this is a very powerful resource and could well serve you.

If you have a clearly defined set of values then this also will help you in making decisions. An example might be having to choose between spending time with your family and time at work. If family is more important to you then you will make sure you spend as much time with them as possible in preference to spending too much time at work.

The greater your awareness about your own life circumstances, your habits, your beliefs, your values and social networks the more you can draw on these resources to make the change process in your life easier to manage.

You can practise new ways of behaving by doing something familiar in a different way or doing something unfamiliar to develop new skills.

2. The principle that imagination is stronger than will

When the imagination and the will are in conflict, generally the imagination wins. For example, think of a man who is perfectly willing to walk a plank raised a foot high off the ground for a sum of money but, if the same plank is placed a hundred feet in the air, stretching across a busy roadway, he will immediately decline the offer because in his imagination he is visualising himself falling down from that great height. As the 'imagined' consequence is so great this can easily overcome his 'will' to carry out the act.

3. The law of reversed effect

In life people often find that the harder they try to do something the more difficult it often becomes. This is mainly because worrying about something interferes with the brain's focus on the desired pattern that it is trying to complete. For instance, if you are learning to dance but arouse another pattern of, say, trying to impress a dance partner at the same time, there is a conflict of patterns that the brain is trying to complete. It can't complete and so you fail at the chosen task. Similarly, if you consciously think too hard about a task, such as tying your shoelaces, that should be carried out unconsciously, you begin to over analyse the action. By over analysing it you are interfering with the 'knowledge pattern' in the subconscious for carrying out that skill.

4. The law of concentrated attention

When attention is focused on an idea or a pattern it tends to happen. This is one of the most crucial ideas that permeates all disciplines (and may even feature in the way reality itself is constructed). There is a tendency for any idea that is focused upon to actualise itself.

5. The law of scatter

If you think about the many different ways and approaches you can use to make changes then the idea of changes is more likely to take hold. Thus, over time, we embed the learning involved in that suggestion much more effectively. The simplest example of this is summed up in this Eastern Proverb

"Tell me and I forget

Show me and I remember

Let me do and I understand"

So if you first tell a person something, then show them and then let them do it they are more likely to understand the idea you are trying to share or teach.

6. The law of one step at a time *(the rule of the first domino)*

"The journey of a thousand miles begins with the first step"

Making changes in your personal or professional life is often just a question of getting the first change started. This then sets up a momentum that brings along a train of other changes in your life. It's been likened to a row of dominoes, balanced close together, when you tip the one on the end of the row, they all fall over. In just the same way, initiating a small change will start off a cascade of changes in your life.

But to every rule there are exceptions. Sometimes it is appropriate to go for a major change but we need to be aware that often a small change is enough, and may even be the most effective way forward.

7. The law of dominant emotions

This states that strong emotions win out over weak ones. If you can create a strong feeling connected with a possible future life event, that provides the energy to propel the change into your life.

For example, if you associate a certain degree of pleasure with smoking, you can create a bigger association with fear about the consequences of smoking on your life. That fear will then win out over the pleasure and help to initiate changes that will make it much easier for you to give up smoking.

8. The rule of positive expectancy

This states that we should expect the best from ourselves and situations.

9. The carrot principle

Choose something that will motivate you. Think about giving yourself a reward after you have completed a desired goal.

10. The principle of positive suggestions

Always focus on giving yourself positive suggestions rather than negative ones. This is connected to the carrot principle.

What the brain can imagine is much more likely to be carried out. So a concrete, positive suggestion such as *"visit your friends more"* is much more achievable that an abstract concept such as *"be happier"*, *"be more positive"*.

11. The principle of positive congratulation

"Keep interest in your own career, however humble.
It is a real possession in the changing fortunes of time.
Enjoy your achievements as well as your plans."

In short learn to enjoy your successes, however small and also congratulate other people in their successes and share in their joy.

You don't have to use all of these principles. You can choose the ones that work best for you and remember you can use the others later if you need to.

All of the methods of motivation described above are ones that were identified by psychologists in the Western World. In the Eastern Traditions of learning and motivation a different method of motivation is suggested and I quote directly from the work of Arthur Deikman[1] so that you can consider this approach and make up your own mind which method or methods will serve you best:

Serving The Task

*When we speak of doing a job well, for its own sake, we refer to a shift of motivation in which we give the needs of the job precedence over our own wishes. We recognise that the proper accomplishment of the task may **call for** a certain amount and type of effort. For example, in writing this book I may be* *aware that a certain passage isn't quite the way it should be; it is not complete, not finished. I can get by with it; it will do, but I feel that it is not the way it deserves to be and am pulled to meet its requirements, even if no one else notices the difference. The pull is not a compulsion but a recognition that the task is not complete in **its own terms**. I may decide that I am unable to do what is required, or that it will not be worth the time or effort needed but, nevertheless, the perception is clear - something more is called for.*

Doing what is needed instead of what you might prefer to do is a choice that occurs in a wide range of situations - intellectual, mechanical, artistic, or interpersonal. In all such instances, the experience may be described as surrendering to the task, but it is a surrender in which the person is active and guided at the same time.

"when all action is dictated purely by place and circumstances"
Huang Po

A. Deikman - "The Observing Self"

The King Who Divined the Future

A King who was also an astrologer read in his stars that on a certain day and at a particular hour a calamity would overtake him.

He therefore built a house of solid rock and posted numerous guardians outside.

One day, when he was within, he realised that he could still see daylight. He found an opening which he filled up, to prevent misfortune entering. In blocking this door he made himself a prisoner with his own hands.

And because of this the king died.

Visualisation

(using the imagination)

Earlier the use of **visualisation** was discussed as one method of stimulating the relaxation response. Visualisation is an incredibly powerful tool and one of the questions you need to ask yourself is: *"What will I be doing differently when I have made the changes in my life I want to make?"* Changes in life do sometimes occur quickly but sometimes it takes a little more time and this is where we bring into play one of your most powerful tools, the imagination.

Practising the task in the imagination

The imagination is like a bridge that makes it possible to carry out the behaviour in real life. Our brains can use imagination to consider possibilities, plan future actions, consider consequences of actions and expand our understanding -.even of the Universe.

It is a common human weakness, however, that we don't draw on this tool enough. People think that, just because they can talk about something, however eloquently, they can *do* it. To think that if you talk about a task it is as good as done is magical thinking.

In terms of change in your life, if you are able to vividly imagine doing something, either for the first time or in a different way, you are more likely to succeed. Activating your imagination through visualisation and then imaginatively drawing on your resources whilst visualising new behaviours will make you *believe* that the change is possible. You need to focus on solution patterns and if you can imagine completing them, you are more likely to do them in the outside world.

Anticipate difficulties

After you've done the visualisation, a very good question to ask yourself is: *"Is there anything I can think of that can occur that might prevent me doing this task?"* By anticipating difficulties before they occur and devising ways around them, you can eliminate any negative suggestions or blocks you might put in the way of completing the task.

It is worthwhile remembering that all changes involve some risk and should be undertaken only after careful study of all facts available.

Ask yourself these questions frequently

- What problem am I trying to solve for myself in doing this?
- Is it working?
- Might there be a better way to achieve the same goal?

4 Principles Of Visualisation

1. Make it real. Think of a previous event or a future event and imagine it in all of its detail. Add the five senses. See the event in as much detail as possible, what do you see, hear, smell and what does it feel like? *Stanislawski* used a method known as emotional memory to help actors recapture an emotional experience from their past and apply it to the present.

2. When you visualise make it a positive experience

3. Make it regular. You need to get into the habit of visualising morning and evening.

4. When you visualise apply it to all things. Successful people visualise before any major event. It is their habit. They see themselves achieving success and making it happen.

When all is said and done just get on and <u>do it.</u>

Life continually presents challenges to all of us. That makes each of us vulnerable to disappointment when important things do not go our way or, worse, when catastrophe befalls us. Though it may sound trite, it is still true to say: *When things fall apart, there is an opportunity to rebuild.* Do you want to just survive life, or transform it into something wonderful?

The first step to managing your life well is to recognise early warning signs that something important is happening that requires your attention. Bad things do not have to grow into terrible things if you react quickly and effectively to curtail them.

Always remember prevention whenever possible is the first and best choice.

PEOPLE SKILLS

Communicating Effectively

Although this book has been divided into three sections I hope that it will be clear to the reader that all of the sections are inter-related and effectiveness in living is dependant on developing the necessary skills and understanding in each section. Therefore it is unlikely that you will develop good 'people skills' if you have not learnt the value of relaxation, developed your understanding of your values, clarified your boundaries, become more familiar with your emotions, recognised your thinking style and its effect on you, become aware of various psychological influences and learnt how to recognise and manage your belief system.

Good communication skills are greatly enhanced with increased self-awareness and with that in mind we can now move on to look more specifically at communication skills

Communication Style

How would you describe your 'communication style'? Do you consider yourself to be a good communicator or someone who is a little more introverted and struggles with communicating with others? Can I suggest that you use the assessment exercise that follows to give you some idea of your 'communication style'?

Rate yourself on a scale of 1 - 10 in the following dimensions

Gregarious		Shy
Flamboyant	....	Reserved
Poised	....	Casual
Spontaneous	....	Controlled
Animated	....	Withdrawn
Self-disclosing	....	Non-self-disclosing
Trusting	....	Guarded
Good eye contact	....	Little eye contact
Friendly	....	Distant/aloof
Varies voice pitch	....	Speaks in a monotone
	....	

People who communicate well seem to be 'natural' communicators. They are people who come across as being at ease with themselves, are natural, sincere, relaxed and they enjoy communicating with other people. They generally have the ability to put other people at ease and are able to communicate their message effectively and easily. The purpose now is to help you develop your communication skills and become a more 'natural' communicator.

Mehrabian (1971) states that 55% of our communication is physical, 38% vocal and 7% is the actual words. We communicate through our bodies, faces, our vocal tone, intonation, pitch, volume and words and all of these are of extreme importance in any communication that we undertake. All of this points to the fact that the actual words we use are of minimal importance. People, generally speaking, do not so much listen to **what** we are saying but to **how** we are saying it.

When developing communication skills you need to be aware that being able to establish good rapport and have good communication skills creates the right conditions for an effective exchange of thoughts and ideas. We all need to pay a lot more attention to **how** we are communicating if we want the communication to be effective.

One of the key ways of managing change in your own life is developing the skills and abilities needed to communicate effectively.

We reach, persuade and motivate ourselves and others with words. However we do not just 'touch' people with our words. We 'touch' people with the sounds of our words, with the emotional content of our words, with our body language and with the energy of our words. To communicate effectively we need to reach people on an emotional level as well as on an intellectual level.

Being unable to communicate effectively can create many difficulties if you are in the process of making changes in your life. If you are making changes and you don't communicate this to people around you it may cause emotional upset and unnecessary arguments or if you communicate your goals or ideas aggressively or with a lack of conviction you may find it difficult to convince others that your intentions are sincere. In both of these instances having poorly developed communication skills could well sabotage your efforts to change. Take the example of Gordon Brown the current Labour leader. Gordon Brown is a well-educated and highly intelligent politician.

However he appears to come across very badly on television and they don't appear to trust him. He looks uncomfortable in front of the camera and appears to lack empathy. Barack Obama on the other hand dresses very smartly, talks and acts with confidence and as a result comes across effectively both as a person and a politician. In short he wins emotionally. I'm sure you can find events in your past where your communication skills failed you.

A very important thing in any communication is to 'touch' a person on an emotional level as well as on an intellectual level. This is equally true when you are going through the 'wheel of change process'

6 .... However a merely intellectual decision is often not enough to drive action.

7.   The **heart joins the head** in the decision. The decision is reinforced by values and emotion and so this 'fuller' decision is more likely to drive action.

A large part of any communication takes place on a sub-conscious and pre-conscious level and you need to be able to get through to yourself and others on these levels. It is also necessary to use emotion in this process:

"...Your sub-conscious mind recognizes and acts upon ONLY thoughts which have been well mixed with emotion or feeling.

Plain unemotional words do not influence the sub-conscious mind. You will get no appreciable results until you learn to reach the subconscious mind with thoughts or spoken words which have been well emotionalised."

Napoleon Hill[1]

Once again it is worth repeating that it's not just what you say but how you say it that matters. There needs to be '**emotional content**' in what you say and you need to 'care' about what you want to do. This is not about losing emotional control. This is about using your emotions in an appropriate manner. The energy of the voice, the physical posture, the emotional state and the rhythm all shine through when we communicate. These same factors also influence your own self-talk.

Hopefully it is now clear that your emotional responses play a crucial part not only in your communications with other people's self-talk but equally with yourself and the world around you.

How you **feel** about yourself and how others **feel** about you affects your behaviour and how you and they **react** to you. Your feelings affect all parts of your life. Take for example when you are buying something. It could be an item of clothing, or a car, or a house. Generally speaking people buy something based on emotion and then they will justify the purchase with fact. We all do. Most of your major decisions are based on emotional reactions. When people buy a house it is usually how they "feel" about the house that most influences them. If this were not true then why are there so many lifestyle programmes on the television and programmes that give you tips on how to sell your house? The advice given will include painting the walls in light "airy" colours, having plenty of fresh flowers around for a nice smell and appearance. None of these changes will affect the price of the house in the slightest but they will affect how a person reacts to the house and how it makes them **feel.** Virtually all advertising is not trying to sell a product based on how good it is. Advertisers employ a whole repertoire of skills including visual, auditory and implied messages in an attempt to get people to buy a product.

The impression you give to people does carry some importance and often people will get a job based on an overall impression. I, myself have experienced the effects of the impression I have given to other people. Some years ago I went for a job and I was more than adequately qualified and experienced for the job. In fact I was one of the two people who had been selected for the final interview. I felt sure that I would get the job but I didn't. When I spoke to one of the people who interviewed me he said to me "You didn't look as if you were too bothered about the job."

Whether you realise it or not you are constantly communicating to people in a multitude of different ways. The emotional and other messages you send are "silent messengers" which reach the sub-conscious mind or the 'emotional centre' and they are very powerful. They have a lot of influence and we all need to be aware of this influence.

Developing Effective Communication Skills

In order to get anyone to **listen** to what you are saying and to consider the merits of what you are "saying" then it is necessary to get access to the higher brain functions. This is where the analytical processes take place. *Goleman*[3] reveals how modern research has consistently shown that parts of the brain are of utmost importance when communicating. When considering the art of effective 'rapport' building and communication it is helpful to understand a little about the brain, its effect on ourselves and its involvement in our responses to the information it receives.

The brain consists of the *brain stem*, the *cerebrum* and the *cerebellum*. The *brain stem* (the reptilian part of the brain) is the **oldest** part of the brain and is responsible for reactions to sensory impulses. The *cerebellum* is **newest** part of the brain that contains our cognitive and reasoning abilities. The importance of this information will become clear later.

Studies in neuroscience have shown that the reptilian part of our brains is almost fully formed when we are born. The reptilian part of our brains combined with the limbic system is responsible for arousal and our "flight or fight" response. There is also part of the brain known as the *amygdala*. The *amygdala* along with the reptilian part of our brains and the limbic system is largely responsible for our "emotional" responses. *Decker*[1] describes this as the *'emotional centre'* and *Goleman*[2] also shares this view and his book 'Developing Emotional Intelligence' goes into great detail to explain how this mechanism works and how to develop it. From now on I will refer to this part of the brain as the *'emotional centre'*. The nerve pathways to this part of the brain are extremely well established and these parts of the brain receive impulses quicker than the newer parts of our brain, the cerebellum (the *"New Brain"*). The *"New Brain"* is responsible for our cognitive functions and analytical thought.

Research has shown that the neural pathways to the *'emotional centre'* are very well established. They date back many millions of years. The messages that are sent along these pathways are also very crude and if they are strong enough then the strength of this signal has the capacity to overcome our cognitive functions or New Brain and we react on an emotional level not a rational level.

Many of the reactions from the *'emotional centre'* are learnt responses from our childhood and therefore largely pre-conscious reactions. When we learnt these emotional reactions we did not have words and so they go largely undescribed and are merely *"feelings"*. Goleman[3] and *Decker*[4] believe that emotions are at the heart of all our actions and that if you want to communicate effectively it is perhaps wise to remember this.

The *'emotional centre'* is, in many ways, the *Gatekeeper* and has the power to grant access to higher brain functions or prevent access to the higher brain functions.

A key aspect in good communication is the ability to befriend this *'emotional centre'*. We need to make this *'emotional centre'* feel at ease so that the message can get through to the higher functions of the brain.

Decker also believes that the *'emotional centre'* understands the language of **TRUST**. The *'emotional centre'*, will therefore exercise a great deal of influence as to whether the messages get through.

As has been mentioned earlier the *'emotional centre'* is connected to the survival instinct. In order to pass this obstacle to the "thinking part of the brain' you need to convince it to accept you as trustworthy and believable.

Through our knowledge of psychology and psychiatry and the research done by *Goleman*[5], *Argyle*[6] *and Cialdini*[7] and neuroscientists it is now well understood that many of the reactions to people are conditioned from an early age. Whether you realise it or not many of the experiences you have in your early years and the effects of such experiences affect you long into adult life. Before you are able to speak, you feel and react on a purely emotional level. A young baby has not developed cognitive functions and so will react on a purely emotional level. The consequence of this is that as babies we will generally learn to associate smiling, happy faces as good because they will leave pleasant emotional memories in the *'emotional centre'*. Other, more traumatic events will leave very negative impressions on the *'emotional centre'*. Therefore when people shout or are aggressive towards babies this will probably leave strong negative emotional triggers, which will be activated if you see expressions on people's faces that have been associated with a negative experience.

The effect of this in adult lives is that if you are sending messages through the use of your body and voice which make you appear boring, anxious or disinterested to another person then generally speaking you won't get through to them.

Therefore it seems clear that it is very useful to know how to use yourself more effectively. You can practise and develop your communication skills. Authors such as *Argyle[8]* and texts on Neuro-Linguistic Programming describe what skills are needed but in the field of vocal and physiological in communication but they talk very little about '**how**' a person can take more control of their own voice and their own bodies. In order to develop a new 'habit' then you need to understand three things. Knowing '**what**' to do, knowing '**how**' to do it and understanding '**why**' you are doing the new 'habit' are three key factors in developing new 'habits'. *Rossi* believes that approximately 3 to 6 months is required for that new habit to establish itself. If one or more of these elements is missing it is highly unlikely that the habit will become firmly established. *Linklater[9]* and *Berry[10]* have written whole books on developing the voice and *Feldenkrais[11]* wrote about how physical and emotional tension in the body can restrict our ability to communicate effectively.

Your vocal, verbal and physiological skills can be **"tuned up"** so that they are able to communicate the messages that you want them to communicate. The only way you can practise and develop your communication skills is by becoming more **aware** of how you use words, your voices and your body. **Self-Awareness** is a key factor to becoming a more effective communicator.

You also need the listener to trust and believe you for the communication to be effective. **Trust and believability are therefore probably synonymous.** If you do not believe a person it is highly unlikely that you will trust them. It is also worthwhile noting that if you do not believe yourself then you will have difficulty convincing the sub-conscious that you mean what you say.

In today's world we are all plagued by telephone sales people. When these people contact us they "recite" their message. It is obvious to any listener that these people do not believe what they are saying and they are certainly not 'emotional centre' friendly. The effect of repeating a speech in such a parrot like fashion is that we do not believe what they are saying and, if we do not believe them it highly unlikely we will trust them. If we do not trust them then we certainly won't buy anything from them. Anyone who works in telesales should remember this fact. Merely reciting words will rarely convince anyone and the seller will usually have little success. A pleasing, believable telephone manner will placate the 'emotional centre' and give you access to a person's higher brain and they will, at least, listen to what you are trying to say.

The way you perceive things, your world-view or your 'frame of reference', also affects how you feel about them and this is a view shared by psychologists who describe it as a *'personal construct'*. *Covey*[12] gives the example of a father boarding a train with several children. The children run about causing all sorts of disturbance to the other passengers and the father does nothing. The passengers are getting increasingly annoyed and eventually one person talks to the parent to express his concern about the children's behaviour. The father, who has been somewhat distracted, apologises and tells the person that they have just left the hospital where the children's mother has just died. This immediately affects everyone in the carriage and their perception of the events. Anger is now replaced by sympathy and the desire to help the father. The paradigm has shifted and the way that the people communicate with the father has changed completely. What this story perfectly illustrates is that we all have different perceptions of the world and our ability to appreciate another persons view will ultimately affect how we communicate with them and hopefully make any communication more effective.

We can all benefit from learning and becoming aware of the language of behaviour. If we are speaking to someone and we hear a quiver in the voice we are generally suspicious. We usually ask ourselves what is causing this person's voice to quiver. A "quivering" voice does not, generally speaking, communicate a message of confidence and self-assurance. Another behavioural habit that creates uncertainty is the habit of 'eye dart'. If a person's eyes dart around and never rest in one place for more than a second the likelihood is that we will be suspicious. Whether we realise it or not we all react to a multitude of signals that is sent out by a person's vocal tone and body posture.

Our most natural communications probably take place when we are talking to babies. As adult's no one is bothered about the noise we make and how we talk to a young baby. We use our voices freely;

make lots of "silly" noises and the expressions on our faces are also very expressive. The way we communicate with a baby will be etched on the brain of that baby. The baby is therefore going to associate smiling, warmth and confidence with good. It will see open, relaxed, unaffected and spontaneous behaviour, as natural, and natural communication is likeable.

If you want to make an impact when you speak then your **words**, your **voice** and your **body** need to have **rhythm, intonation, tonal variety** and **emotion**. When you have an expressive voice you will create interest. When your voice lacks rhythm, intonation, tonal variety and emotion you will, more than likely, *'turn off'* any listener.

Consider this example. Have you ever been to a talk where the person giving the talk uses lots of hand-outs. They also have a *whiney* voice. If you have ever been to a talk like this, and I have been to many, you probably won't be very interested and you will switch off.

Or, if you are at a talk and a person uses lots of acetates for the over head projector or lots of slides, or the latest trend in using Power Point Presentations. They are in a darkened room and have a flat voice. You probably won't be very interested. Perhaps you have heard of the expression "death by OHP!" and one that I have coined from seeing too many Power Point Presentations - Power Point Paralysis. The overuse of any visual aid combined with a lack lustre performance by the speaker is a recipe for **boredom**!

Behaviour that is perceived as 'boring', 'wrong', 'irritating', or 'annoying' will usually **'turn people off'**. Whenever you meet someone or see him or her for the first time the emotional part of the brain is the first to react. It is chattering away as to whether or not to trust you. In order to establish a relationship with others and convince yourself you need to establish **trust**.

If your aim is to establish trust you have to convince the 'emotional brain' that what is proposed is not a threat and there are many things you can do to achieve this aim.

There are two main factors to consider when communicating with people and these are **the Visual** or **Eye Factor** and the **Energy Factor.** You should not forget the **olfactory sense** is also directly linked to the 'emotional centre' and also plays a significant part in how you react to people. In the Western World the perfume industry is massive and personal hygiene has become a major industry.

The Eye Factor

As has been mentioned already the **visual** connection is the beginning of most communications. The visual impact that a person makes has perhaps the greatest impact. In today's world you are surrounded by visual images from the media and through these your visual senses are bombarded. Consider the impact of television and the popularity of video games. These impact directly on the visual sense and advertisers spend millions creating a "company image" that will capture the imagination of the public. Consider the Nike "swoosh" and the three stripes of Adidas and the Apple logo for Apple computers. All of these are instantly recognisable and bring to mind all kinds of associations. Whether you like it or not the visual image is very powerful and leaves a lasting impression on everyone who is exposed to it over and over again.

Most people will agree that the spoken message has a lot more impact than the written word. In communicating the spoken message the importance of the various elements of communication have been studied and the figures widely touted for each part of the communication are as follows.

Words - 7%, **Vocal -** intonation, projection, resonance and voice 38%, **Visual -** what people see. Emotion and expression that people see when you speak 55%.

I hope that it is becoming clear from what is written above that the **visual factor** is of extreme importance.

When you communicate with someone the more the above factors are in harmony the better your message will get across. Words - Voice - Delivery and rational argument all need to be in harmony and you need to do what you can to avoid mixed messages.

WYSIWYG is a computer term and means, "What you see is what you get!" It is perhaps useful for anyone who wishes to communicate to another person to remember the WYSIWYG formula because it sums up nicely the effect of the Visual Factor. For many people what **they see** is what they believe **they will get**. With regards to communication the challenge then is for any communicator to develop their 'Visual' skills and the skills involved in the 'Energy Factor'. These skills can only be developed by the communicator becoming more self-aware and working on themselves to develop the necessary skills.

There are four skills involved in the Visual or Eye Factor:

1. Eye Communication
2. Posture and Movement
3. Dress
4. Gestures and Expressions

Eyes

Eye contact is extremely important in any communication and eye contact is also like **mind-to-mind** contact.

In order to establish effective eye contact with a person you need to engage eye contact for approximately 5 seconds. This length of time is important because you want to create involvement rather than intimacy or intimidation. It is generally agreed that 5 seconds will create involvement rather than intimacy or intimidation. Intimacy and intimidation mean you look at the person for more than 10 seconds and this can make people feel uncomfortable. If people feel uncomfortable they are highly unlikely to trust you and the communication will probably be unsatisfactory.

Argyle[13] suggests that 90% of contacts call for involvement. If you wish to test yourself count to 5 and maintain steady eye contact before looking away. You also need to be aware of problems such as eye dart. Eye dart is when a person looks away after a short period of time and their eyes are constantly moving from one place to another. They never hold their attention on one spot for more than a second or two. Avoiding eye contact in this way can often be interpreted as fear or lack of confidence. Try doing it yourself and make a note of how it makes you feel.

It is also wise to beware of the slow blink. In this case a person closes their eyes for a couple of seconds. This can suggest boredom or suggests that you really don't want to be here.

If you wish to develop your use of the eyes then you might want to try some of the exercises on the following page

Exercises

a. Practise 1 to 1 keeping track of eye contact - silently counting to yourself or have a 3rd person watching who will do the counting.

b. Practise with a paper audience. In this exercise you place pieces of paper on chairs in different parts of the room and you ensure that you spend time focusing your attention on the pieces of paper for approximately 5 seconds.

c. Stick notes on chairs and hold your look for 5 seconds on each part.

Posture and Movement

Do you know what messages your body is sending out? Does it communicate confidence or does it communicate fear or insecurity? The most powerful messages you send are those that come from your posture and your use of your body. The way you use your body. Remember what was said earlier 55% of communication is through our physiology. The authors of books on Neuro-Linguistic Programming go into some detail about the importance of body language and how good communicators can 'match'[1] other people's body language and use this skill to establish rapport and therefore communicate more effectively. Others have considered the use of the body as so important both to our health and our ability to communicate that they have developed their own theories on how to release these tensions. Consider the work of *Feldenkreis[1], Alexander[2], Reich[3]* – a former student of Freud who developed the theory of "Character Analysis" using the body and *Lowen*, a student of *Reich*, who developed Bioenergetics to explore the link between our bodies and our minds.

To develop the ability to use the body more effectively and, as a result, develop more self-awareness you may have to spend some time practising and learning the necessary skills. The aim of developing physical awareness is to enable a person to use their body in a totally natural and unrestricted manner.

---

[1] If you would like to learn more about 'matching' then look at 'NLP in 21 Days' by Alder and Heather

"To make any movement, certain muscles have to have tension. What you do not want, however is unnecessary tension, because all unnecessary tension is wasted energy - it is energy being kept in and not made available for communication. This means that you have to be aware of the separateness of muscles and what they do..."

Cicely Berry:1979 "Voice and the actor"

Berry wrote the above when she was writing about the voice, how to "free" and develop it. All actors, who read these words, and who have received any form of voice training will recognize their importance. These words however may be unfamiliar to other people who, as part of their daily lives, communicate with others. You do not, however, only communicate with the voice; you also communicate with your body. It is of little value if you say one thing through the voice and the body communicates something differently. To use the words of Shakespeare an actor should attempt to:

"Suit the action to the word
The word to the action.
With this special observance
that you o'erstep not
The modesty of nature."

Hamlet

Let's look at how you can develop an awareness of the body. Just as the voice needs to be understood, practiced and maintained, so too does the body. Anyone involved in communication should understand the need for vocal exercises and they should also understand the need for exercises that will free the body of tension and allow them to use it to communicate effectively. A relaxed, flexible, agile body can be of enormous benefit to anyone who wishes to communicate more effectively. Through it they will be able to express more clearly what they are trying to say and there will be harmony between the body and the voice and the person will be able to express a much greater emotional range.

"An actor must take care that his muscles are completely free from any strain whenever the part demands particularly strong emotional action."

'Stanislavsky on the Art of the Stage'

A neglected body can be a clumsy instrument. Muscular tension, reinforced by habits, whether they be emotional, physical or mental can seriously limit a person's ability to express themselves and will have a profound effect on the messages that the person is sending out to other people. Unless a person can become aware of these tensions and can free themselves from such burdens, then they may well be condemned to being misunderstood and sending out the same messages throughout their lives. voice coaches would probably agree that it is virtually impossible to free the voice if the body is full of muscular tension.

When making changes in your personal or professional life the ability to communicate effectively to those around you is of great value. People are put in all kinds of different situations both in their social lives and in their work lives. Each situation has its own demands both on the person's voice and on the body. It would therefore seem logical to suggest that the greater the knowledge and awareness a person has of their physical self the greater will be their ability to use it to its best effect whatever situation they find themselves in. Whether that be talking to themselves, their partner, a friend at work or giving a formal presentation.

The *'emotional brain'* can pick up the slightest doubt, the smallest movement, the smallest gesture, and that action can express countless words or add weight to the words being spoken. Alternately an incorrect or exaggerated use of the body can make the communication look, insincere, unnatural, wooden and unconvincing. Anything that allows a person to develop their physical self and their physical awareness can therefore only be of benefit in the process of change.

So how do you develop this awareness? Many people do exercises so why bother with anything else. The answer is quite simple. Most people will spend many hours going to exercise classes and performing a series of exercises. Throughout this training they often do not know why they are doing these exercises, what muscles are they supposed to be stretching, or how to stretch. As a result of going through an **"automatic"** process like this they will learn very little about physical awareness and how the body works. Such training is a wasted opportunity. There is no reason why exercises cannot be used in the same way as voice training is used by an actor to practice and heighten **awareness of the physical self**. Releasing the body also helps to release the voice. The two are indivisible, inseparable and ultimately have to work in unison if a person is to have any real success in communication. Muscular tension will restrict breathing and movement, strangling the voice and affecting your ability to express yourself physically

"what you do not want is unnecessary tension." **C. Berry**

Developing Physical Awareness

"The habit of relaxing the muscles must be acquired by daily systematic exercises. The muscle controller must become part of the person's own mind, second nature."

Stanislavsky on the Art of the Stage

The development of physical awareness can be undertaken by anyone prepared to devote time and energy towards it. There are however, certain factors that get in the way of developing physical awareness and these need to be considered carefully.

There are three types of habits that can interfere with physical awareness and development

- Behavioural e.g. working, eating, sitting.
- Physiological - breathing, circulation.
- Mental - emotional / perceptual habits that cause stress

Excluding any medical conditions we are all able to have control over our bodies. The problem lies in whether it is conscious or unconscious. Habitual patterns in behaviour, exercise or thinking can, and do lead to increased stresses, which are often aggravated by exercise. These stresses will continue to occur unless we become aware of them and through this awareness learn to change them. The development of physical awareness is not simply doing physical awareness exercises to stretch muscles and perform exercises. The person has to **pay proper attention** to what they are doing and **understand** what they are doing if they are going to receive any real benefit from these exercises.

Physical exercise without awareness can easily lead to injury. The boom period of high impact aerobics is an excellent demonstration of stretching without awareness and many people paid the consequences for such an attitude to exercise. Human beings have many anatomical irregularities and if these are ignored then they will inevitably lead to numerous problems and injuries. These problems can be overcome if a person becomes aware of balance, proper alignment, and posture and has some knowledge of anatomy. The key to good habits in exercise is understanding what we are doing wrong and also knowing how to correct any mistakes we may be making.

Communication is not only about the voice it is also about the body. It is a complex process and this process changes depending on the material you are using. The aim is clarity. Too much tension; physical, mental or vocal will interfere with this clarity. The communicator should not try to over compensate for areas of insecurity or weakness. The aim should be to be true to oneself and to be sincere when communicating.

"Freeing" the voice and the body leads you to being in a state of alertness and readiness."

Linklater

Fundamental Principles

There are five fundamental principles that any communicator needs to bear in mind when performing physical awareness exercises to develop their physical awareness and these are

- Breathing
- Posture/Alignment
- Concentration
- Stretching/ Movement
- Discipline

Breathing

Breathing is necessary for life. The oxygen we take in is needed by all the tissues of the body, including muscles, to remain healthy, provide the energy required and keep the body alive. Starved of oxygen muscles and organs will cease to function correctly and therefore work less efficiently. The first thing that is affected when a person is under stress is their breathing. It will usually become shallow and focused in the upper chest area. Learning how to breathe correctly will keep these tissues healthy and functioning at their optimum level.

Anyone who has received any form of voice or singing training will be aware that breathing is a key factor in "freeing" the voice. Breathing is also important in developing physical awareness. People frequently make the mistake of holding their breath while exercising or under stress and this only leads to increased tension and, as mentioned earlier, increased tension is what we are aiming to eliminate. The exercises for breathing used in voice training are just as relevant when developing physical awareness.

Breathing, using the 7:11 technique also aids relaxation and helps during stretching. Relaxed muscles will move and stretch far easier than tense muscles.

Posture / Alignment

Too many people are **trapped** by their bodies and so the physical mannerisms and presence they carry with them on a daily basis means that they will use the same range of gestures, carry themselves in the same way and so end up sending the same 'silent messages' every time they communicate with other people. This means that people are often stereotyped by others and it is very difficult for them to break such an impression. A person with hunched up shoulders because of muscular tension is communicating tension and this tension will be recognised by the 'emotional centre' and will interfere with a person's message. Such physical tension restricts not only the body but the voice as well. Tension in the neck will constrict and possibly strangle the voice making it sound thinner and hoarser. This is fine if it is what you desire but can be disastrous for the voice if you have no way of relieving such tension.

For those of you familiar with the *Alexander Technique* or the *Feldenkrais Method* you will be familiar with the concept that efficiency of movement is a major factor contributing to good performance in any activity whether it be acting, sports or everyday life. Each activity has specific motions and this is why an understanding of a particular technique, the mechanical abilities and the limitations of the whole body are all part of a proper training and physical awareness programme. Educating yourself about the physical shortcomings of the body requires **self-perception.** In a rush to do an exercise too many people think that doing the exercise is all that is required. It would be far better if people realized *that it is not what you do but how you do it that is important.*

What does alignment mean? A person who always walks with their feet turned out will probably have a mis-alignment stemming from the hips or knees. This will affect their posture and use of the body and so acts as a physical restraint on any action they perform.

Stretching/Movement Technique

The importance of physical awareness is now being recognized in all fields of physical activity. Sports medicine, for example, is a relatively new science and recognizes there is a correct way as well as an incorrect way to stretch. There is now a more thorough understanding of the mechanics of stretching and this has led to changes in the way stretching is taught and practiced. Slow gradual stretching as opposed to the rapid ballistic stretching of old is considered to be far safer and it has been proven that this method of stretching achieves far better results when developing physical awareness. It is also less dangerous and you are less likely to injure yourself while stretching in this way. Such knowledge is equally applicable to anybody who performs movement exercises in whatever form of training and so it is perhaps wise to share the knowledge in one field that is applicable to the training of an actor or dancer.

There are four rules when stretching and these are:
- Stretch should be gentle and slow and held for 10 - 30 seconds
- Do not lock your elbows or knees backward as this hyper-extends the joints and may threaten the integrity of the joint
- The stretch should be felt in the belly of the muscle. You do not want to feel the stretch in the tendons or the ligaments.
- You must be aware of the whole body and not just the muscles you are stretching.

All of this may sound very simple but changing habits is very hard. The benefits are that correct technique will ensure more years of healthy activity and also aid in developing awareness.

Concentration

To perform any form of exercise, including movement/physical awareness exercises correctly relies on concentration. You **must** pay attention to what you are doing. No part of your body is unimportant, no motion can be ignored. Such a statement should be self evident to an actor. It is necessary to have some awareness of one part of the body in relation to another to avoid creating unnecessary stresses. Too often people get into the habit of ***"doing"*** the exercises without really **thinking** about what they are in fact ***"doing"***. Concentrating on the exercises will help you to ensure you are performing it correctly.

Discipline

Communicating, sport or educating the mind to the physical shortcomings of the body and exercising requires discipline. At first things are difficult but with practice comes progress. Just as there is a need to set aside a certain amount of time each day to go through voice exercises there is equally a need for time for movement/physical awareness routine and this requires discipline. The discipline required involves setting aside such time and also ensuring that when one does an exercise one does not cheat. You pay attention to what you are doing and how you are doing it. When one is confident in performing the exercises it is perhaps a good idea to combine them with voice exercises and therefore reinforce the point that communication involves an integration of the whole body and is not just restricted to the head and voice.

Combining concentration, breathing, stretching and discipline can help you to integrate the mind and body. This will be of help in any activity whether it be emotional, mental or physical and this level of awareness will also help you in any changes you are making in your life. As someone who works in the fields of health, education, business and the arts it is my experience that such an integration can only help.

Performing physical awareness exercises is something that can be undertaken by the individual once they have learnt the fundamentals of the exercises. Often people's perception of what they are doing does not match with what they are actually doing so it is very useful to have an experienced professional supervising.

The benefits of developing physical awareness are considerable and include:

- You will appear and be more relaxed both physically and mentally.
- Maintain the body in better physical condition
- Reduces stress and anxiety
- Improve co-ordination and balance
- Increased awareness of the body
- You will have increased movement and mobility
- Helps prepare you mentally and physically for any activity you undertake
- You will communicate more effectively

"Muscular tension interferes with the actor's inner work and particularly with his attempts to enter into the feeling of the part. Indeed, while physical tension exists, it is a waste of time talking of correct and delicate feeling,"

Stanislavsky on the Art of the Acting

The benefits of physical awareness are great and as C. Berry says:

" you are looking for the energy in the muscles themselves, and when you find the energy you do not have to push it out, it releases itself. You do not have to push your emotion out, it is released through the voice (and Body). When you can tie this up with your intentions as an actor you have found what you are after, a unity of physical and emotional energy."

Berry:1979 (Voice and the Actor)

Dress and Appearance.

The first 4 seconds are critical in any communication. People tend to form a judgement based, initially, on emotions and then seek to justify this judgement with the rational part of the brain. Therefore if you make a poor first impression even before you open your mouth it may well take a long time to overcome any damage or it might even be impossible to overcome the impression given.

Dress and appearance can be used to communicate who you are! They communicate values, our identity, beliefs about our self-respect and ourselves. Everyone needs to be aware of the messages that are being communicated. We all need to be aware of how they make a relationship with another person.

It's not just about how you are but also need to be aware of culture and values of your listeners. 90% of the body is covered by clothes. 10% is left for face and hair and generally an audience is focused on your face and hair. An impression of who you are and what you stand for will therefore be gained from how you groom yourself.

With regards to beards many people appear not to like them. People often believe that people with beards are trying to hide something. Take a look around you and see how many of our politicians have beards. How many prime ministers in the UK have had beards?

Basic Rules for Dress

Talking about dress is a sensitive topic for many people and some will refuse to alter the way they dress. They consider it to be a 'sell out' or a compromise too great. The question you might want to ask yourself is "What is your intention when meeting another person?" If your intention is to communicate with them then you should be prepared to remove any obstacles that might get in the way of you getting your message across. By way of general guidelines it is important that you dress 'appropriately'. Appropriate both to the environment and to yourself. We all want others to feel comfortable with us and to feel comfortable with ourselves. We need to feel relaxed. It therefore makes sense to choose clothes that you feel comfortable in.

Dress and groom at the conscious level and beware of your habits. We all get into habits of wearing certain clothes and pretty soon our dress sense will become obvious to others and people will categorise us. When we dress for any occasion it might be worthwhile thinking about where you are going and what impression you wish to create.

With regards to jackets it is suggested that you button your jacket. For men, jackets are tailored to be buttoned, and it generally it looks better when they are buttoned. For women wearing a jacket unbuttoned is generally accepted as appropriate.

Exercises

    a.   Ask for feedback from others and ask for honest appraisals of the way you dress and the clothes you wear. Be sure to ask people you trust to be honest with you.

    b.   Be observant. Spend a little time keeping up to date with current fashions and remember to 'dress for success'. Learn from others. The aim here is not to copy another person the aim is to be the smartest you.

    c.   Good dress will make you appear more confident and give a positive impression. It is easy to change your clothes and your appearance will instantly say something about you to other people

Gestures and Smiles

The vast majority of people feel very uncomfortable with gestures. Most feel they are over exaggerating when if fact they are not. This feeling of exaggeration is related to an overall lack of physical awareness and our feelings about using gestures. It is extremely difficult to over exaggerate a gesture. You will not over exaggerate a gesture if it is appropriate to what you are saying.

Here are a few tips on gestures and smiles. Open arms are welcoming. When a person stands with their arms folded it is interpreted as a defensive posture and the 'fig leaf' posture is one that is commonly associated with nightclub bouncers.

The smile suggests openness and likeability. If you want to experience the power of the smile then I suggest you visit Thailand – "the land of the thousand smiles". The Thai people smile so naturally and so genuinely that you would have to have a heart of stone not to be affected by the warmth of a traditional Thai greeting.

Body gestures reveal our inner state. If we fumble about nervously or move our hands about nervously or constantly repeat a gesture it says something about us and generally makes any listener feel uncomfortable. Effective communication can only be enhanced if you learn how to gesture naturally. Gestures should always be natural and you should feel comfortable with them. Always try to be honest and sincere to yourself and do not force a gesture. As was mentioned earlier *"suit the action to the word and the word to the action."*

Developing Gestures

It will help you to improve and develop your gestures and facial expressions if you consider the following:

- Find out your habits when making gestures
- Find your nervous gestures.
- Remember that in most cases it is difficult to over-exaggerate.
- Smile!

Exercises

1. Practise with a partner.
2. Count your nervous gestures.
3. Role playing
4. Watch TV with no sound.
5. Test your smile.

Benefits

There are many benefits to developing your gestures and these include being able to express your thoughts more fully. Smile and the world smiles with you. A lot of energy can be released when you smile. The use of open gestures show your openness and willingness to listen. You will be able to emphasise important points with ease when you are in the habit of using gestures and smiles. Use movement and energy in gestures when appropriate.

Remember that the **visual sense** is perhaps the most dominant sense. The **visual factor** rules the language of the *'emotional centre'* whose language is one of emotions. If we learn to communicate more effectively using our eyes, paying more attention to the way we dress, our use of gestures and our general body language we will be able to reassure the 'emotional brain' that we are not a threat and so gain the trust of the listener.

The Energy Factor

There are four parts to the Energy Factor and these are:
1. Listening and developing empathy – 'Circle of Attention'
2. Voice and vocal variety.
3. Words
4. Humour.

Listening and developing empathy – 'Circle of Attention'

There are different degrees of listening and these can range from a passive uninvolved level of listening to a very involved intense level.

There are also different ways of listening. When you are listening for facts you are using the 'thinking brain' which deals with information. Many people try to use this method when listening to new information.

Decker[1] describes one level of listening as **feeling listening** which he considers to be an active and multi-channel listening. Others describe it as **empathic listening** and Co-Active Coaching[2] describes this 'global' listening as **Level III** listening because you are not only listening to the words, you are listening to what is behind the words, to the intonation and the emotion and you are taking information in from all around you including the environment. Level III listening involves making Emotional Brain to Emotional Brain connection through **eye communication**. It involves being receptive to everything that is going on. Getting to the feelings behind the facts and what is said.

When you are listening at this level we acknowledge feedback by your responses to the speaker. by acknowledgement, nodding, gestures, body language, words, reflection.

Real communication is always a two way process. An effective communicator is always responsive to the cues he receives from the person talking to you or from the audience. Listen when you talk, when you listen, listen with your whole body. When people feel they are being listened to this in this way then they feel they are truly being listened to.

You have to listen with your eyes and your heart. Can you remember a time when this happened to you. If you can then you will realise what a powerful experience being listened to really can be.

Probably the most precious gift you can give another person is your attention and to listen to them 'attentively'. On the surface this probably appears to be something very simple and yet so many people feel they are not listened to. In this section the purpose is to look at how to develop your listening skills and also how to give someone your attention. A useful way of looking at this is to look at the *'Circle Of Attention.'* This is an expression which is taken from the world of acting. More specifically it is taken from the work of *Constantin Stanislawski* who was the originator of 'Method Acting.' The term *'Circle of Attention'* refers to the area of concern a person is concentrating on. In general terms there are three 'Circles Of Attention' and depending on the level a person is operating on will determine the quality of their listening and the quality of attention a person is giving to someone else.

On a **physical level** *Egan*[3] suggests that there are five things you would be doing if you were giving someone your full attention and he uses the acronym *SOLER* to sum these up:

Physical attending

1. *Facing the other squarely*

2. *Maintaining an 'open' posture*

3. *Leaning toward the other*

4. *Maintaining good eye contact*

5. *Remaining relatively relaxed.*

On a **psychological level** a person would be:

'Listening' to non-verbal behaviour which means being aware of how the person communicates through the use of their face, body and gestures.

Listening to verbal behaviour – listening to the way the words are used, voice, intonation, the feelings and the experiences the other person expresses.

The first level of attention is when one person's main focus is on themselves and what they want to say and not really listening to what the other person is saying. Typically a conversation with this type of person would go something like this:

A: Where did you go for your holiday?

B: Oh I went to the Costa del Sol and it was really beautiful and…

A: Oh the Costal del Sol! I've been there. It's beautiful isn't and the weather is so good too.

B: Yes and the food was very nice and …

A: The food!!! I love Paella and all the seafood. It's fantastic and I also love Sangria. Did you visit anywhere?

B: Yes we went to Sevilla and Granada and when we were there we…

A: I've been to Sevilla and Granada too. The architecture is fantastic and the Alhambra Palace in Granada was beautiful and (so on and so on)

As you can see from the above **A** is more interested in his own experiences rather than learning about the experiences of the other person and spends little time listening to what **B** has to say. The two people involved in this conversation are clearly not communicating and **A** is certainly not listening to **B**. **A** hears the words of the other person but the focus is on what it means to him. Therefore if these two people were in a room their focus would be on themselves and involved with their own worlds as shown in the diagram by the circle that surrounds them and there is no connection between the two.

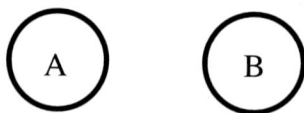

Fig 1

Level I In Fig 1 the two people, A and B, are focusing their attention only on themselves and so 'real' communication would be difficult.

Level II Listening - Empathy

If you look at the diagram below you will notice in this case that **A** and **B** are connected and sharing some of their 'space'. In this situation **A** is trying *to get into the world* of **B**. On a physical level he would probably be facing **B**, the eye contact would be better, the posture more open, leaning in and possibly more relaxed. When **B** spoke he would spend more time listening and showing that he is listening by nodding his head, giving verbal signals that he is listening such as 'really', 'ah-ah', 'tell me more' and other comments like this to show that he is interested and wants to learn more about the experiences of **B**.

Conversations at this level may well sound like the following:

Sue: I'll never get a job transfer .

Marie: You're feeling really frustrated.

Sue: Yeah. Everywhere I go they tell me to leave a resume, and then they never call me back.

Husband: I don't want you to play cards tonight.

Wife: You don't like me having fun without you.

Husband: It's not that. It's just that I want to be alone with you tonight

Level II Listening

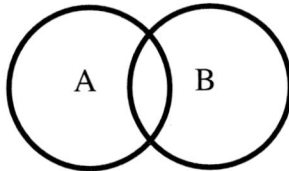

Fig 2

Level II - In Fig 2 A's 'Circle of Attention' is connected to B's and A is clearly focused on B. The circle of attention now includes them both as illustrated by the circle which encompasses them.

Level III Listening

Wider Environment

Immediate Environment

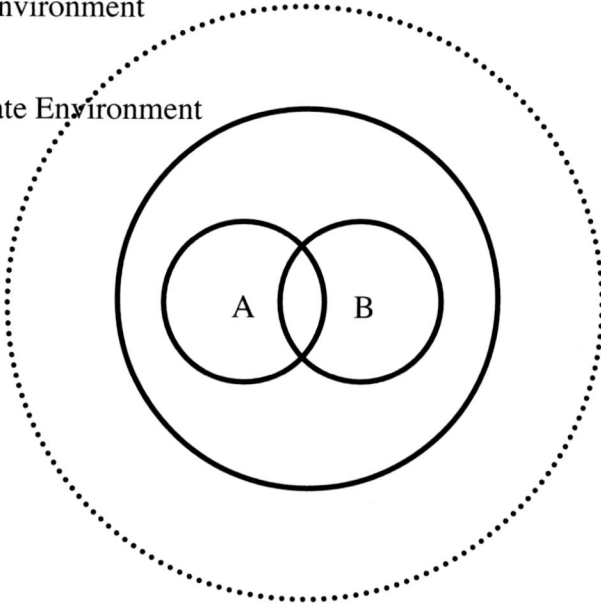

Fig 3

Level III Listening – Deeper Empathy

At this level of listening **A** is not only trying to understand **B's** point of view he has also extended his 'Circle of Attention' and depth of listening to try and understand the *implicit* information that **B** is unable or unwilling to communicate. Level III picks up everything else including intonation, emotion, mood, pace and energy, the impact of the immediate environment and also the impact of the wider environment outside of the room.

In order for a communicator to get as much feedback as possible it is preferable if they are able to operate at Levels II and III. Level III is the highest possible level of awareness and will give the greatest amount of information.

Examples:

A: *I write a lot of verses – I'm not sure I should call it poetry. My friends tell me they like it, that it's good. But then they're not critics, they're not experts at all. I keep writing and keep sending it off to various magazines and all I get back are rejection slips. This has been going on for two full years. I could paper my bedroom wall with them.*

Level II response: *It's disheartening to put in that much work with so little success.*

Level III response: *It's disheartening to put in that much work with so little success. It maybe even makes you wonder about your talent, and you don't want to kid yourself.*

A: *I really don't think that I can take my boss's abuse any longer. I don't really think she really knows what she's doing. She thinks she is doing me a favour by pointing out what I do wrong all the time. She has no idea that she comes on patronising and even abusive. I like the work and I'd like to stay, but, well, I just don't know.*

Level II response: *What makes this really frustrating is that your boss might not even realise what she's doing to you.*

Level III response: *The alternatives, then, are limited. One is to stay on the job and just 'take it'. But you feel that this has become too painful. Another is to talk with your boss directly about this whole destructive relationship. A third is to start thinking about changing jobs, even though you like the work there. We really haven't talked about the second or third possibilities.*

Listening at **level III** makes a lot more demands on the listener and requires more focus and concentration. The listener really has to 'tune in' to what the speaker is saying and also what he is not saying and respond in such a way that it reflects a deep understanding of what the speaker is saying.

Voice

You transfer your strength of feelings and attitudes through your voice. Actors and singers will spend many hours working on their voices so that they have control of how they communicate their feelings and attitudes through their voices. You can communicate a lot merely through the use of one word. If you doubt this statement then listen to a person on the telephone and what have you learnt about them from the moment they say "Hello". Also it is worth bearing in mind that if you cannot see the person the energy and emotion of the voice, the Vocal Aspect, accounts for approximately 80% of the communication.

You need also to remember that how we hear ourselves is not how the listener hears us and this is because we hear ourselves through our head and not how others hear us.

We can all remember examples of people whose voices are dull and boring and the impact that this has on the listener. Everyone has been to a presentation or a lecture where the person delivering the talk has spoken with a dull monotone voice. The result of this is an instant 'switch off.'

The challenge then is to find ways to develop your use of the voice and there are many ways to develop the voice.

Here are just a few tips:

- Make the voice naturally authoritative - learn a speech or a poem or some short quotes.

- Put your voice on a roller coaster. Use its full range. Practise using a sentence or by counting from 1 to 10.

- Be aware of your telephone voice. Is it different? If so why?

- Get into the habit of putting real feelings into your voice.

- Is your voice flat? Be conscious of emotional signals you are sending when you speak to a person with a 'flat' voice.

Four basic components to the voice

Relaxation

Hopefully you are beginning to realise that there are recurrent themes in this book and 'relaxation' is one of those themes. The ability to relax and remain calm is of the utmost importance in developing all areas of your self and your ability to live your life effectively.

Breathing

Breathing and relaxation are closely bound together and learning how to breathe properly is of enormous benefit to you both personally and to all areas of your well-being.

Projection

Filling the Space. Projection is not a term used by many people in the acting profession. The reason for this is that the word projection implies forcing the voice outward. *Berry* and *Linklater* prefer to ask the speaker to merely think about the space they are trying to fill. Therefore if you are in a small room you will speak accordingly and if you are in a large auditorium the awareness of where you are means you will fill the space naturally. The speaker is working from the inside out. The thought drives the breath and then the voice will be produced to accommodate the space.

Resonance

Each of these elements can be worked on and I encourage you to learn and use poems and speeches to develop your voice. A couple of poems have been included in the Resources Section of this book and I encourage you to use them or to find others that you can find useful.

Words – 'Vague' Language

A good knowledge of language is of great value when communicating and contributes in many ways to living more effectively. You use language to bond and co-operate with others, exchange information and to try to convey your thoughts and feelings. As you do this you may also, through your choice of words, convey unconscious thoughts and ideas. Experienced and effective hypnotherapists make common use of 'vague' or 'hypnotic' language and use it to communicate powerful messages directly and indirectly into their client's world.

Whether or not there is a true justification for the use of this language will be discussed later but for now I suggest that you study 'hypnotic' language, become familiar with it until you understand why, how and when it is best used. This type of language is used knowingly by therapists and unknowingly by all of us and so you need to spot when it is being used.

Be aware / Beware of nominalisations (reification)

Nominalisation is the linguistic term for an abstract noun which is produced by taking a verb or adjective and making it into a noun.

e.g. The verb *to depress* is turned into the noun *depression*. The verb *to fear* is turned into the nominalisation *fear:*

To do something successfully is turned into the nominalisation *success.*

To enlighten somebody about something is turned into the nominalisation *enlightenment.*

This process of nominalisation is important for you to observe and understand. This is because, when people use a nominalisation it always means that essential information is deleted: namely, precisely *who* is doing precisely *what* to precisely *whom*. To fill in the missing gaps in the information when we hear a nominalisation, we have to search our own memory and identify what we believe are matching experiences from our own past to give meaning to these words when someone says them to us. They are word snares that can trap and destroy us if we let them.

If you are not aware of nominalisations they can affect you emotionally and mentally and can seriously affect your effectiveness in living and communicating with others

It is important to be aware of nominalisations and challenge them when you feel it is necessary. A simple test to identify a nominalisation is to ask yourself, "Can I see it, touch it or carry it away?"

Nominalisations are considered to be a powerful 'tool' of communication and can be used for good as well as harm. Consider the following example used in a therapeutic context:

*'You have many more resources for better **communication** than you are **consciously aware** of You are so full of **creativity** and, by focusing your **mind** positively, you can **integrate** those **resources** and you may be surprised to discover the **healthy changes** you can start to make and the **joy** and new **insights** they can bring. "*

The person, in this case, has to search and discover their own meaning for the above nominalisations because they are non-specific. Because *they* choose the meaning, it is argued, that the meaning is more motivating for them.

There is an extremely important point to be aware of here. The other person, through their use of language, is attempting to 'manipulate' the other. This person will be unaware of how powerful these terms are and may well be influenced by this use of language. As an individual you may well have to ask yourself whether or not is justifiable or right to 'manipulate' another person in this way or in any other context. Some will argue that we all attempt to manipulate each other and so it is therefore justifiable for all of us to do it. I'd like to draw your attention to a quote from Dr Michael Yapko when he wrote the following on manipulation:

*"The chief problem with manipulative tactics is that while they may, in the short run, enable you to get what you want from another person, they allow you to **devalue** that person. In essence, you're saying, "Getting what I want is more important than how you feel." Such tactics work against the longer-term health of the relationship by hurting the self-esteem of the other person. You've probably learned this from your own experience. If you have ever had someone lay a guilt trip on you, you know that you felt not only guilty, but also angry that the person would manipulate you. It didn't help your self-esteem to feel you were being used."*

Clearly Dr Yapko does not favour the use of 'manipulative' language or tactics and all of us need to consider when, where, how or if we should use such language to manipulate others. If the aim is to stimulate someone's imagination, or generate debate or possibly help someone in a therapeutic context then their use may well serve a very useful purpose. If however the aim is to confuse, manipulate or cover up your inability to communicate effectively then I would question their use. Tony Blair once famously said that he believed in "Education, education, education!" All well and good but what, in fact, does it mean. Politicians, advertisers and sales people make wide use of such language and I would offer the view that their purpose is not to clarify something, it is there to confuse and hide the true intent.

So, with that in mind, remember to familiarise yourself with 'nominalisations' so that you can spot them when they are being used and use them or challenge them as, and when, you choose to do so. To help you become more familiar with 'nominalisations' here are a few of them to consider.:

Fun, happiness, purpose, connection, grounded, earthed, spiritual, security, health, well-being, attention, professional, success, depression, stress, achievement, balanced, commitment, love and quality.

Take some time to look at each of these words and then write down what each word means to you. You might also find it useful to ask other people what these words mean to them. You might well be surprised by the answers you get.

Words, Non-Words, the Pause and Silence

"The difference between the right word and the almost the right word,
is the difference between lightening and a lightening bug."

Mark Twain

Although the words we use may only account for 7% of the total communication you should not forget that words we use are, as discussed earlier, of enormous importance.

It is very helpful if we have developed the ability to use the right word for the right situation. Unfortunately in many conversations or talks far too many of us fail to give due consideration to the words that we are using. People use words very casually and this is a common cause of misunderstanding. Think of all the arguments that happen in which the crux of the argument is based on what was said.

"But you said you were happy!"
"That's not what I said!"
"That was the word you used?"
"But it's not what I meant". And so on and so on.

Words do matter and we all need to be aware of the words that we use if we wish to communicate effectively.

The effect of using the right word can be seen in any great poem or speech. Consider the impact of any great speech:

"I have a dream ..."
"Our greatest fear is not that we are inadequate
Our greatest fear is that we are powerful beyond measure".

Using a different word can have a dramatic effect on the impact of a sentence. "The Ten <u>Suggestions</u>" would carry a significantly different meaning to "The Ten <u>Commandments</u>".

A great deal has been said in many self-development books on Positive Affirmations and the use of our vocabulary. *Black*[1] and *Robbins*[2] to name but two. Affirmatations include statements like: *"every day in every way I'm getting better, better and better"*; or *"everything is coming to me easily and effortlessly"*, or *"I love and appreciate myself just as I am"*. With regards to positive affirmations *Zeus & Skiffington*[3] offer the following view:

> *"Despite exhortations in numerous self-help books to constantly recite positive affirmations, we can waste or expend much energy telling ourselves that we feel great when indeed we feel terrible. It is more helpful to stay with the "terrible" feeling, experience it boldly, and then to examine and challenge any faulty beliefs that may be contributing to the feeling."*

The key thing to point out here is that our faulty beliefs may have a far greater impact on us than positive affirmations and it is the faulty belief that needs to be dealt with. The theory that is offered in many self-help books is that what we say will affect how we feel about ourselves and we are encouraged by such authors to use affirmations and to become aware of our vocabulary and to choose words that are more dynamic and positive. The suggestion is that certain words have negative impact upon us and repetition of such words will reinforce that negative impact.

I am not in total disagreement with this opinion but I would like to offer the view that the words we use should describe the way we feel. No word or words should be off limits to a person. If we restrict our vocabulary we restrict the ways we are able to express the way that we feel at any given moment. The aim for any person is to use the appropriate word for each situation and to be aware if they are 'limiting' their vocabulary in any way.

Restricting our use of language may eventually affect our thoughts and our actions. We all need to think more carefully before we speak and we also need to expand our vocabulary so that it will reflect the richness of human emotions and experiences.

We all need to develop a feel for words and a love for language.

1. **Build your vocabulary.** The English language is rich and is filled with synonyms. There are many thousands of words to choose from so that you can say what you mean and mean what you say.

Compare the use of :

meticulous	with	**careful**
pivotal	with	**crucial**
endow	with	**give**
disciple	with	**follower**

Always be on the look out for new words.

2.   **Paint word pictures** - metaphors and vivid expressions create memorable impressions on the 'emotional centre'. Examples of such language include:

"To soar like an eagle."
"To float like a butterfly."
"Like a knife through butter."
"Make hay while the sun shines."
"Life is a bowl of cherries."
"He had a burning desire to succeed."
"What you are saying is music to my ears."

3.   **Beware of Jargon!** Every profession seems to have its own 'jargon'. There is nothing more likely to 'turn off' a listener than the overuse of 'jargon'. Of course the use of 'jargon' is context dependent but always be aware that the listener may not have the same educational or professional vocabulary as you. When people don't understand 'jargon' they rarely challenge it, they just 'switch off' and a 'glazed' look will appear in their eyes.

Non-words.

A non word is a "word" or expression that someone repeatedly uses and because of the overuse it carries no real meaning. We all have a tendency to use non-words when we are nervous or we use expressions that have become part of our speech.

• *Eh.., Ah.., um...*

All of these words will block your message. Also expressions like:
You know what I mean?
So.
Actually.
And then
You understand, don't you?

The over use of such words and phrases will make you appear incompetent and nervous.

It is important that you recognise your non-words and eliminate them from your vocabulary. Learn to listen to yourself and replace non-words with something more powerful – **the pause**.

The Pause

"The most important part of speech is the pause."

Ralph Richardson

The pause and the silence are key parts in all the plays written by Harold Pinter. In his plays more is *"said"* in the pauses and silences than could ever be spoken with words. Consider the following exerpt from **"The Caretaker"**

DAVIES: This your room?

ASTON: Yes.

DAVIES: Must be worth a few bob, this ... put it all together.

            Pause.

            There's enough of it.

ASTON: There's a good bit of it, all right.

DAVIES: You sleep here, do you?

ASTON   Yes.

DAVIES: What, in that?

ASTON: Yes.

DAVIES: Yes, well, you'd be well out of the draught there.

ASTON: You don't get much wind.

DAVIES: You'd be well out of it. It's different when you're kipping out.

ASTON: Would be.

DAVIES: Nothing but wind then.

            Pause.

ASTON: Yes, when the wind gets up it ....

            Pause

DAVIES: Yes ...

ASTON: Mmmnn …

Pause.

DAVIES: Gets very draughty.

ASTON: Ah.

DAVIES: I'm very sensitive to it.

ASTON: Are you?

DAVIES: Always have been.

Pause.

You got more rooms then, have you?

The Caretaker page 11

The dialogue is minimal and there are a lot of pauses and …. I hope that you will agree that the pauses create a lot of dramatic impact and tension and also show that there is a lot of thought going on in these periods of pause and silence.

The purpose of this sample of dialogue is to encourage any communicator to use the power of the pause and the silence. Pause for up to 3 seconds. If you are worried about pauses then you might want to remember that behind every pause and silence there is a thought process going on. You do not have to fill all the space. A pause gives the listener time to think and it gives you time to think. Pauses and silences also create impact.

Humour

Humour is an extremely useful tool to use when communicating with another person. However it needs to be used wisely. Humour creates a bond between speaker and audience. People like to be entertained and it helps them to relax and it gets in touch with the first brain.

One of your aims should be to make the formal informal by using humour.

"When you stand up before an audience you should speak to them as you speak to other men and women in daily discourse. Be you own natural self."

Carnegie

Basic rules for using humour

- Don't tell jokes. Leave comedy to the comedians. It takes a special skill to tell a joke.

- If your joke fails the 'emotional centre' will shut down and you have lost your listener.

- Fun is better than funny. Create an atmosphere

- Find a form of humour that works for you. What's your type of humour? Can you use stories and anecdotes from your life?

- Use the humour in language. Emphasise the right words. Eg Ageism "prejudice against the elderly by the temporary young."

Benefits

- More likeable, and listeners will have more fun. Everyone will have more fun and you will have a lot more energy in your life.

- People like people who put their conviction into motion expression and variety in language. All the communicative energy is there inside you waiting to be released.

Always keep in mind that the person or people you are talking to are not your audience they are your listener.

Self Development Of The Emotional Centre

We have spent sometime discussing how to communicate effectively with another person and how to become *'emotional centre'* friendly so that our message(s) can get through. We also need to be aware that we too have *'emotional centre's* and that our own *'emotional centre'* can exert a powerful impact upon us. As has already been discussed the *'emotional centre'* is related to our 'Fight or Flight' response and these emotional signals can exert very powerful influences over us. One of the most powerful influences is FEAR. Fear can be all encompassing and paralysing and we need to develop our ability to cope with fear.

Fear

"It is not because things are difficult that we do not dare. It is because we do not dare that they are difficult."

Seneca

It is extremely worthwhile exploring the power of your own *'emotional centre'* which, when understood, can transform your life for the better. Brought under the control of the conscious mind you can use the *'emotional centre'* to help you.

One *'emotional centre'* fear is the irrational fear of public speaking. Public speaking frightens many people. In a survey done by *Decker*[1] on communications 41% of people said public speaking was their number one fear. In order to disarm this fear you need to know where it comes from, how it affects you and what you can do to control it. Why is public speaking the largest fear that affects people? This fear limits us and affects our potential.

The fear has its genesis in the way the *'emotional centre'* works. When we are in a potentially 'dangerous' position the *'emotional centre'* will send off many powerful fear signals. Actually it is many fears bundled together. Broken into its component parts it is known as performance anxiety.

Fear of speaking brings up three main fears and these are:

* Fear of exposure
* Fear of failure
* Fear of criticism

These fears can be so overpowering because they are *'emotional centre'* fears. The *'emotional centre'* is unreasoning, sub-conscious and related to our instincts to survival. The *'emotional centre'* does not reason or analyse it reacts emotionally to threats and danger and this will release chemicals that cause many physiological responses. The 'fight and flight' response. The effects of the 'fight and flight' response will be:

* Increased pulse rate.
* We consider we have only two options and these are the freeze and fight response or flight. This survival instinct used to serve us well in the past but it doesn't now.

- Raised blood pressure
- Move it or lose it.
- Sweating
- Pupils will dilate.

You can't reason with your *'emotional centre'* and you can't limit its responses but there is a way to bring it under control. We can teach our New Brains to stop shouting danger at our *'emotional centre'* and imagined threats. Through the use of our cognitive functions we can teach the brain the difference between real and imagined threats.

Many people who feel confident about telling you something when sitting down in an informal situation will find it considerably more difficult if you ask them to stand up in front of a group of friends and then tell them about the same things.

What happens to people in this situation? It appears that their perception of the situation changes and people feel they are *presenting* rather than *talking* to people. People suddenly begin to feel that they are being judged, that they look foolish and that they may be criticised. Once this happens the signals from the *'emotional centre'* flood the system and we lose control.

What is it people are afraid of when talking in front of people? Is it embarrassment, judgement or is it failure? All of these sound horrible but do we really have so much to fear from other people. Our fears are magnified in our minds. If we are able to take a rational and objective look at the situation then we can see that we are not judged or criticised half as much as we believe we are.

Psychologists have done a lot of work on the development of self-esteem and found that when an individual actually attempts something in the vast majority of cases the individual succeeds. However if the individual does not make the attempt they have an impression of failure. As a result of this most people perceive themselves as failures due to the fact that most of the time they do not make the attempt.

By not making an attempt at something we create the belief that we are not good enough, and if we believe we are not good enough then we will not make an attempt. A negative self-belief has been formed and this cannot be broken unless we take risks and discover that what we "believed" to be true is not so.

Hornay discovered that 95% of the time we succeed at what we attempt to do. If you can adopt the attitude that if you fail at something then you can learn from it you will go some way to overcoming the fear that you have. Perhaps it is worthwhile asking yourself why you should sacrifice every performance for the sake of that 5% risk of failing. That is what most people do. With this knowledge you now have some insights that can help your new brain quell the effects of your *'emotional centre'*.

- You know that your physical survival is not at stake.

- You know that you have little or anything to fear from the judgement of others.

- You know that the odds are in your favour.

- You know that you are better than you think you are and the best is yet to come!

- FEAR according to Ziglar is an acronym for **F**alse **E**vidence **A**ppearing **R**eal. What we perceive as a threat isn't really a threat but we can convince ourselves that it is a real threat.

The *'emotional centre'* is a powerful source of energy. It is like a live firehose that is not being held by anyone. It moves about wildly, swinging in all directions, unpredictable and enormously powerful. Imagine this is the emotional energy that drives you. The *'thinking brain'* is like a fire-fighter that has the capacity to take hold of the hose and then use it in an effective way. In effect the *'thinking brain'* takes control of the *'emotional centre'* and can direct its energy where it wants it to go. Once under control this energy can be directed in the way that you want to direct it. It is under your control.

We need to remember that we no longer live in mortal danger of our lives and the "fight and flight" response does not have to control us. *Buscaglia*[2] claims that 90% of what we are worried or frightened of never happens. We have the ability to control our *'emotional centre'* responses.

Public Speaking

Public speaking means pressure and speaking under pressure is one of the most important things that we do. We need to be able to channel this energy to work for us and not against us. That is what all top performers do in athletics, business and theatre. We never want to completely eliminate performance anxiety because it creates dynamic tension. There is a line between dynamic tension and fear, and it is a line that we do not want to cross. The butterflies that we feel prior to a performance are good. They help to keep us on our toes and to keep us alert.

Decker[3] outlines **four stages** of speaking and suggests that you find out which one you are in so that once identified you can go beyond it.

Non-Speaker – the emotion of terror. The speaker is scared of standing up in front of people and displays extreme shyness and very passive behaviour. They generally have a low skill level and work in jobs that don't require speaking or communicating. However as they progress up the ladder the non-speaker is called upon to speak some more and moves into:

The Occasional Speaker – the dominant emotion here is the emotion of fear. The fear is not paralysing but the fear shows. This type of speaker can be coaxed into speaking but doesn't feel comfortable speaking. They feel reluctant but are aware that communication skills are important. Their position is that of the front line doer with a growing ability. The occasional speaker is not locked into terror and with more practise can become:

The Willing Speaker – the emotion for this speaker is tension with a hint of 'fight and flight'. This type of person finds the speaking environment challenging. They will state their view at meetings. They have butterflies in the stomach but they fly in formation. Their position is usually management. As they become more practised and more comfortable with speaking they will become:

The Communicator – the emotion is one of stimulation and excitement about speaking. They enjoy the occasion and the feedback. They enjoy speaking and know the rewards to be gained from being an effective communicator. Their position is one of leadership. They are able to motivate and inspire people.

The good news is that whatever stage you are in you can move on if you are willing to devote the time and energy on practise to develop your communication skills. One of the ways that you can prepare yourself for speaking is by using visualisation.

Eye communication

Without good eye contact it's like listening to a stereo system with one bad channel.

Tips to develop your listening skills

- Use your eyes.
- Nod your head when appropriate.
- Open posture leaning in.
- Make vocal responses.
- Clarify if necessary.
- Reflect, paraphrase and give feedback
- Respond at the emotional level. Touch if necessary.
- Feel it don't fake it.

- All this must be real and sincere.

Willingness to listen to someone is probably the greatest gift we can give another person. *Rogerian Therapy* is based almost wholly on listening. If people do not listen then they will not succeed in communicating. Have you ever been in the situation where someone's trying to sell you something and you want to leave. They continue to push the sale and keep you there. They don't realise that you want to leave. The longer they keep you there the more you want to leave and the less you want to buy. The harder they push, the harder you resist. A sale will never happen and the person selling could have saved themselves a lot of time if they had **listened** and realised you wanted to go.

Level III listening, as discussed earlier, is about making an emotional contact with the other person and indicates care, respect, understanding and even love of the other person.

To acknowledge someone you let another person talk and you are sensitive to how they feel and what they want to say. You do not argue, explain or try and cheer them up. You do not try and analyse, you allow the person to speak. When people have something on their minds they just want someone to listen. People are in process and they need to clear their heads. Often when they have gone through this process they feel better. This process applies just as much to a group as it does to an individual. Consider the group dynamics and acknowledge the group and adjust your approach accordingly. Listening to acknowledge is about First Brain contact with a person. When using this level of listening you are listening to the level below. It is therefore wise to:

- Ask questions gently
- Be empathic and understanding
- Listen to yourself - do you feel yourself getting annoyed - level 1 listening
- Continue to listen and ask until a "soothing" moment has been reached.
- Try to be an objective 3rd party listener. Use the skills of coaching. Set your own agenda aside.

When feelings have been acknowledged and cleared then you can come back to facts. The 'thinking brain' must be in control of the "emotional centre" before you can carry on. Feelings must be under the control of reason.

"The brain must control the blood"

Nelson Mandela

When you are listening to another person you need to bear in mind that there is no absolute truth. You are listening to get at the other persons truth.

"The heart has its reasons which reason knows not of."

Pascal

When you are **level III** listening the whole process takes time and one needs to accept and acknowledge this fact. It is of vital importance that you give the other person the opportunity to say what they want to say and so move through and out of their present emotional state or state of being. It is foolish to try and force a person through this process. Sometimes people just need some time to 'clear' their mind and so be ready to move on. The best thing that another person can do is just listen and give the person the space they need.

Other Factors

When considering communication there are certain other factors that have great significance and give one great insight and clarity. Some people call these Aha! moments or EUREKA moments! A time when everything seems to make perfect sense. Here are just a few of those moments.

Dr Maltz[4], a plastic surgeon who worked with people with physical deformities and performed many operations. Throughout his career he changed their bodies but he realised that he didn't change their minds. People who felt they were unattractive before an operation still felt unattractive after the operation.

Maltz[5] came to the conclusion that people who feel bad about themselves continue to feel bad themselves. They limit themselves in many way and the more we limit ourselves the less we think of ourselves and the more we will limit ourselves. People set in motion a circle of negativity which is difficult for them to break and self-limiting beliefs are reinforced due to this thinking process.

He believes that the vast majority of people do not have the power to see themselves objectively. When you are able to look at yourself with greater objectivity and recognised your own self-limiting beliefs you have reached eureka moment number one. At this point you can look at your self-limiting beliefs, examine them and then replace them with more positive self-beliefs based on a new perception of reality. The old way of looking at yourself can be left behind and you are now in a position to move on. If you have not already read the poem by Nelson Mandela then I ask you to read it and consider its meaning.

Our greatest fear is not that we are inadequate

Our greatest fear is that we are powerful beyond measure.

It is our light, not our darkness that most frightens us.

We ask ourselves

Who are we to be brilliant, gorgeous, talented and fabulous.

Actually who are we not to be.

You are a child of god

Your playing small doesn't serve the world.

There is nothing enlightened about shrinking so that other people won't feel insecure around you.

We are born to make manifest the glory of God that is within us.

It's not just in some of us, it's in everyone.

And as we allow our own light to shine, we unconsciously give other people permission to do the same.

As we are liberated from our own fear, our presence automatically liberates others.

Nelson Mandela - 1994 Inaugural Speech

Feedback

The aim is to become a more skilled communicator and skill is a collection of habits used to perform a task. In order to develop our skills we all need some feedback. People function on feedback and feedback will help us to grow. There are basically four types of feedback

- People feedback
- Video
- Audio
- Self-feedback - self-awareness.

People Feedback

We all like positive feedback but if we are given too much positive feedback then we may consider it to be insincere and it will not have the desired results. Negative feedback is generally destructive and is de-motivating. Our aim in giving feedback should be to enable people to learn, to develop and to enhance their performance. The nature of the feedback therefore has to be delivered with care and consideration for the person's feelings.

We can ask people to give us feedback but we should also ask that they deliver it in a certain way and this kind of feedback should consist of **3 strengths** and **3 distractions.** Do not use the words **positive** and **negative**. We all need balanced criticism to thrive and change.

Audio feedback

There is a proliferation of audio recording devices and we can all use these to get some instant feedback on how we sound. I suggest that you get in the habit of using it whenever you can. Through the use of audio feedback you will get used to hearing your own voice and become more aware as to whether or not you are saying what you think you are saying the way you want to say it. Treat the tape recorder as your friend as it can provide you with valuable information about yourself.

Video feedback

Camcorders are now relatively cheap to buy and so it is in the realms of everyone to buy one and use to give themselves some instant feedback on how they are coming across to other people. With a camcorder you are in a position to video a talk or presentation and become your own "director".

There is one danger in the use of video and that is the fact that you are working from outside in and not inside out. We need to "feel" that what we are doing is right. Video can tell us if what we think we are doing is what we are actually doing. The use of video has to be handled carefully because in the wrong hands video feedback can be very destructive.

Self-Awareness

One of the most important forms of feedback is that gained from our own self-awareness. The more we learn about ourselves and the more we are able to look at our behaviour objectively the more we will be able to learn and the more we will be able to change our own behaviour.

Disparity

There is a marked disparity about how we feel about ourselves and our performance and how other people perceive our performance. The way we feel is often not the way we come across. Communication thrives on energy. Passion and energy increases communication. A person cannot just release emotional energy. You can tell a person as much as you want to do something but unless they can experience it for themselves it means nothing

People need to develop awareness visually, emotionally and experientially. An example can be when you ask a person to move around a stage who is not used to moving. You can ask people to experiment with their gestures. At first they will feel uncomfortable but with experience they can see, feel and experience that it works and is very effective. *Adler & Heather*[6] describe the process of learning very effectively. They break it down to four stages:

Unconscious incompetence - we are unable to do something and we don't know it.

Conscious incompetence - we are now aware that we are not able to do a thing.

Conscious competence - we have learnt a new skill but have to think about it.

Unconscious competence - we now have mastery and no longer have to think about performing the task. It has become instinctive.

In many cases the disparity is all between our ears and if we can break the connection between how we feel, and how we are, we will be able to perform to the best of our ability.

Downey[7] described it thus:

Fulfilling Potential - a new possibility

Potential   **Performance**

Potential - interference = Performance
   (minus)   (is equal to)

If we can eliminate or minimise the level of interference or disparity between what is real and what we perceive as real then we are in a position to maximise our communication. Remember a person only gets what you give them. They may not know how nervous you are, or how you feel or what you are going to say. They may know nothing about your background and they don't know if you have missed a word out or made a mistake. Only you know these things and only you can communicate these things to your audience.

In any form of communication the goal is *free and natural communication.*

Mental Agility - Thinking On Your Feet.

Mental agility is the ability to speak spontaneously and without notes. These skills can be learned and used. The more we know about our subject the more we are able to be spontaneous. Spontaneity is grounded in confidence and knowledge. Often when we speak we get bogged down in accuracy and we should be focusing on power and spontaneity. Whatever we are talking about and whoever we are talking to we need to bring it alive. Consider David Bellamy, Billy Connoly and Barack Obama. Here are speakers who have tremendous energy and tremendous enthusiasm for their subjects. Once again remember that the listener only gets what you give them.

Informality, spontaneity and wit are all products of the New Brain. Many of us are frightened of speaking because we are afraid of looking like fools and because we have this fear we block our spontaneity. Overcome the fear of speaking to people and you will be in a position to be more spontaneous, more natural and more at ease with yourself.

You can develop your mental agility through practise. The more you practise the more experience you will gain and the more comfortable you will feel. Practise gives us experience and greater skill. Skill and repetition give us confidence. Confidence gives us the ability to be more natural and more relaxed.

We also need to learn how to "be in the moment." When we are "in the moment" we are focused on what we are doing at that particular time and not worrying about something about something that has happened or will happen. We are totally focused on the **here and now**. We are process orientated and practising the philosophy described in Buddhism and Taoism. Also known as 'flow'…

You can practise these skills. All you need to do is to welcome change and be flexible. Focus on what you are doing and only on what you are doing at any given moment. With practise the ability to operate in the here and now will develop.

Trust the power of the pause. You won't ramble or freeze but it will give you thinking time and dramatic effect.

Prepare. The more you know your subject the greater the knowledge you will have to draw on as and when you need it. Always have a focused point of view.

Another, very important thing to remember is to <u>trust yourself</u> and go with the flow. Remember you are better than you think you are and trusting yourself will allow your natural abilities to flow and shine through.

Trust Your Mind

To sum up, remember the following points:

1. Don't read a speech.
2. Have a strong point of view
3. Trust your mind.
4. Be in the moment
5. Don't worry about transitions.
6. Be confident - inner game of communications is when your mind runs free.

"Whether you think you can or you think you can't, you're probably right."

Ford

Confidence Equals Mastery.

Our confidence will grow the more we do something and the more we do something the greater our mastery and as we gain more mastery we gain more confidence and so and so on.

Confidence in yourself attracts confidence from others. The better you can communicate the more comfortable you will be with yourself and the more comfortable other people will be around you. You will become a natural communicator and your 'rapport' building skills will become more effective.

Mastery of the Natural Self

When we express our natural selves we become effective communicators.

We need to be aware of our strengths and weaknesses. We can develop our strengths and also work on our weaknesses. The aim is to bring the natural self out to the fore again. We are not learning something new, we are learning to be our natural selves. Get in the habit of analysing your own strengths and weaknesses.

"Beyond a wholesome discipline be gentle with yourself."

Ehrmann

The aim of any self-analysis is not to be too hard on yourself. The aim is to be honest with yourself and to recognise your strengths and weaknesses. Always write down your strengths as well as your weaknesses. Do not paint a negative picture of yourself. The aim of the analysis is to help you to develop not to make you feel bad about yourself. Celebrate your strengths and develop your weaknesses.

Once you have identified your weaknesses then try and change one thing at a time and not everything at once. If you do too much at once you may well fail. It is always better to work on one thing at a time before moving onto the next thing to work on.

When we can master ourselves we will be able to connect with the 'emotional centre' of the listener. Building confidence is easy but you need to take risks and to move outside of your comfort zone.

"There is no growth without risk."

Buscaglia

8 Steps To Transform Your Skills

It is probably clear by now that everyone has the ability to develop their communication skills and the development of these skills can be summarised below. Once a person has spent the time understanding and developing their communication skills they will be able to put them to good use in whatever situation they might find themselves in.

1. Think 'emotional centre' and make it a part of your mindset.
2. Know your strengths and weaknesses.
3. Focus on one skill at a time.
4. Speak at every opportunity.
5. Get feedback every chance you get using the 3 x 3 rule.
6. See yourself on videotape for objective feedback.
7. Take risks
8. Just do it.

"Each time we ask more of ourselves than we think we are able to give. We manage to give it and then we grow."

Decker

Goals! Goals! Goals!

"Do you want to be a wandering generality or a meaningful specific?"

The Fisherman

In a small Portuguese coastal village, a fishing boat was returning to port. An American, who happened to be on the pier, complimented the fisherman on the good quality of his catch and enquired how long had he been at sea.

The fisherman replied *"Not very long."*

"Well, why didn't you stay at sea and catch even more fish?"

asked the American. The fisherman said that he had caught enough for his needs.

The American then asked, *"But what do you do with the rest of your time?"*

"I sleep-in every morning, I fish a little, I play with my children, and I spend as much time as possible with my wife. In the evening I go to the village to see my friends. We drink port or iced beer and talk about the people coming and going in the village. In fact, my life is quite full."

The American interrupted him: *"I have a fantastic plan for you! I have a Harvard MBA and I can show you how to get rich. You should start by fishing for a little longer each day. With the extra revenue, you could buy a bigger boat and be able to catch even more fish!"*

"With the even greater profits, you could buy a second boat and so on until you own a fleet of fishing boats! Instead of selling your catch to a middleman, who reduces your profit, you could directly negotiate with the fish processor or better still, open your own cannery!"

"Then you can leave your small village and move your offices to

Lisbon and from there to L.A., or even New York! From there you could direct all your businesses and expand globally."

The fisherman became thoughtful and said at last, "Well, your plan of my career is interesting. How much time will all this take?"

"10 or 20 years," replied the American.

"Really?! And then what?"

"After that?! This is where it gets interesting!" replied the American smiling with his perfect white teeth and laughing, "When that moment arrives, you float your company on the stock market! The sale of your stock to the public will earn you millions!"

"Millions! And then what?"

"Well, once have made your fortune, you could retire, reside in a small coastal village, sleep-in every morning, play with your children, go fishing for a while, take an afternoon nap with your wife and spend the evenings drinking and chatting with your friends..."

It may appear to you a little strange to find the discussion on 'goals' at the end of the book. The reason for this is quite simple and based on the view that far too often people set off to achieve their 'goals' without taking enough time to consider the desired goals and whether or not they possess or have acquired the necessary skills and abilities. This is often a recipe for frustration, confusion and ultimately failure. We are all encouraged to set goals and most people usually think only about 'having' goals and 'doing' goals. They often forget about the 'being' goals. 'Having' goals will include things like: having the new house, the new car, the holiday, the plasma screen TV and the new clothes. 'Doing' goals may include exercising regularly, going out for meals, to the theatre, to concerts and doing many of the things they wanted to do. However, many people discover, that even though they have the things they want and are busy 'doing' things they are still unhappy, ill at ease, perhaps with a sense of anxiety, apprehension or worry and end up with a nagging feeling that something is 'missing' in their life. People may well think about what they want and where they want to be but far too often they forget to think about the 'how.'

The how is not just about the practical steps they may have to take but how they will be as a person. If you go about achieving your goals in an impatient, selfish and intolerant way then it is highly likely you will still be impatient, selfish and intolerant after you have achieved the goal. People forget to think about goals that are related to the kind of person they are and developing qualities like *patience, tolerance, compassion, kindness, generosity* are ignored or just do not come into the person's awareness. Developing the ability to listen, to be empathic, to have clarified, boundaries, to know their core values and to have developed their inter-personal skills are aspects of behaviour that are ignored or forgotten. The 'what','where', 'which', and 'when' receive a large amount of attention but 'how' you are as a person and the 'why' often receive little or no attention. Stephen Covey wrote:

"Who you are is far more important than anything you say or do."

Too many people get wrapped up in the *'saying'* and *'doing'* and forget to develop *'who'* they are. The better you understand and develop yourself the better able you are to choose and achieve goals that truly are meaningful to you and to the people you care about. If you don't do this then you are in danger of meeting the fate of *Dave (not his real name) who was married to a beautiful woman and had two lovely children. Dave wanted to be a millionaire by the time he was 40. So, he worked the 18 hour days, 6 or 7 days a week. He spent many days and weeks away from home developing and building the business and sure enough he reached his goal at 40 and sold the business. He thought that everything would be fine. Unfortunately after 3 weeks of retirement his wife left him and took the children and his world collapsed. To her he had become a complete stranger and they barely knew each other. He had missed all the major developments in the growing up of his children. Dave missed their first words, their first steps, their school concerts and numerous parent's evenings. All because he was so focussed on his goal of becoming a millionaire. He was last seen drunk in a pub and alone. He was a stranger to his wife and children and had no idea how to communicate with them. He thought he could talk to them the same way he spoke to people in business but his wife would not tolerate that kind of behaviour and left! Dave had spent no time understanding himself or developing his relationship with his wife and children and didn't know how to relate to them. He has now realised that he needs to develop his interpersonal skills and that he is now doing.*

Dave learnt a very painful lesson and for that reason much of this book has been written with the aim of helping the reader to understand themselves better, to understand others better and have the communication skills required to help in achieving their desired goals.

The ability to set and achieve goals for yourself is, in many cases, affected by your past experiences and your future expectations. If you have had experience of setting yourself goals and then failing to achieve them, the mere thought of 'goals' may create feelings of guilt, bitterness, regret or resentment. All of these feelings may prevent you from setting yourself goals because you may not want to experience them or failure again. If the feelings are too strong they will interfere with your whole experience of achieving your chosen goals and it could well be a very unpleasant one.

If, on the other hand, you focus too much on achieving the goal and the final outcome, then this could provoke unease, anxiety, stress, tension and fear. People can focus so much on the final goal that they become more concerned with the 'end' and less concerned with the 'means'. They may well achieve the desired goal but at what price to themselves and others around them.

It is important to remember that 'goals' have many facets and when you are working towards a goal it is certainly helpful to know where you are going and what you would like to achieve. However it is essential to remember that the most important aspect of any goal is the step you are taking at this moment.

Each goal has, in essence, an outer purpose and an inner purpose. The outer purpose is to arrive at your goal or destination, to accomplish what you set out to do, to achieve this or that. But, if your destination, or the steps you are going to take in the future, take up so much or your attention that they become more important to you than the step you are taking now, then you are completely missing the goal's inner purpose. This has nothing to do with the future or your destination or when you will achieve your goal or where you are going or what you are doing, but, as mentioned earlier, everything to do with the *how*. It has nothing to do with the future but everything to do with the quality of your awareness at this moment. The outer purpose belongs to the horizontal dimension of space and time, the inner purpose concerns the development of your awareness and your development as a person.

Whether or not you reach your goal is, in some ways irrelevant. If you reach your goal but have paid no attention to the how and your development as a person you may achieve 'outer riches and inner poverty'. On the other hand if you have paid attention to the how you may fail completely in reaching your goal but you will have developed substantially as a person.

The sooner you realise that reaching or achieving goals cannot give you lasting fulfilment, the better. Goals are necessary and useful because they give you something to focus on but the destination is not necessarily the most important aspect of the process. The journey and how you arrive at your goal is far more important than the destination.

E Tolle - "The Power of Now"

Setting goals

With the above in mind lets now look again at the 'Life Situation Assessment', you completed earlier. This assessment gives you an 'overview' of where you are at the moment in various areas of your life and your current emotional state. As you look at those scores you may become aware that there are areas in your life in which you'd like to make some changes. If, however, everything in your life is how you want it to be then congratulations! You don't need this book so why not pass it on to a friend?

If you've identified areas in your life where you'd like to make some changes then you are now ready to move onto the next stage of the process. You now need to choose some goals. Any discussion of goals can often cause a wide range of emotional reactions. There seems to be a lot of confusion about goals and for some people setting a goal can cause difficulties. With this in mind lets begin by choosing some goals and the following exercise will probably be helpful.

Take 5 – 10 minutes to write down how you'd like to be, all the things you'd like to have, or do. Take a sheet of paper and divide into 3 columns as shown below and see if you can come up with a list of 50 things and feel free to write anything you want to. You can use the table below as a starting point.

Goals Exercise

Divide a piece of paper into three columns as shown below and then write as many goals as you can in each section. If it helps you can further divide the goals into various sections as shown in "Life Situation Assessment". For example you can have the general headings of Health, Environment, Career, Fun and Recreation and so on.

Be	Do	Have
Be more patient	Run a marathon	A new car
Be kinder to others	Go on holiday	Some new shoes
Be more generous	Get up at 7 am in the week	A new job
Be more tolerant	Exercise regularly	A plasma screen TV
Develop compassion		

(copy the headings and continue on a separate sheet)

After you have completed the exercise above then take some time to think about the following points.

When choosing goals it is useful to think about **what** goals you wish to set yourself, **how** you will achieve the chosen goal and **why** you have chosen that goal.

Is the goal **short term, medium term** or **long-term**.

Be, Do or Have. Goals, as shown above, can be divided into three main categories. These are goals relating to how you want to **be,** goals with regards with things you want to **do** in your life and goals concerning things you would like to **have.**

Goals can be **general** or **specific**, related to how you want to be as a person, for example *"I want to be a patient and compassionate person."* They can be related to what you want to do in your life; *"I want to be an engineer/doctor/teacher/footballer* and what you want to have in your life; *"I want to have a new car/house/holiday/camera etc."* Some goals are easy to define and others require a lot more thought. It is generally accepted that goals that are specific are easier to achieve and, as a general rule, always be as specific as possible when expressing a goal. As a starting point you may begin with making general statements as you did when you first looked at the *'Life Situation Assessment'*:

"I'm not very fit."

"My diet is terrible."

"My finances are in a mess."

"My relationship is going badly."

"I'm unhappy with my job."

"I don't have many friends."

Some of the goals you choose will be easy to achieve and others will require more time, effort and the development of the necessary skills. For your goals it's worth considering the S.M.A.R.T. approach.

(S)Specific Goals - The first part of the S.M.A.R.T. approach is to choose **specific** goals which will help you achieve the desired result. Having specific goals is essential for the following reasons:

• to provide a positive focus for change.

• to be in tune with how the brain works. The brain is a problem solving organ. It needs concrete goals to work towards to mobilise conscious and unconscious resources otherwise it remains trapped in recycling past problems, instead of moving on.

Goals should be stated in a positive manner - It is important to think in terms of goals that can be expressed **positively** and are **specific**. So, instead of accepting *'wanting to be happy'* as a goal, you need to discover how you will know when you will be happy. What will you be doing? Who will you be doing it with? Perhaps you will have new friends, a new job, be able to speak in public whilst staying calm and in control etc. If you express goals negatively then you need to restate the goal in positive terms. So, if you say to yourself, "I want to stop feeling so miserable," you need to ask yourself, "What **do I do** that makes me feel happy."

Goals should be related to needs rather than wants - A **well-formed goal** includes identifying which 'needs' are not being met in your life and then ensuring that they are met. For example, if you are low because you are shy and lonely and have no friends, focusing on looking at goals that will hook you back into society to get the need for friendship and intimate relationships met is probably a very useful thing to do. So it is not just a matter of writing down goals but getting yourself to actually employ social skills in the real world.

(M)Measuring Effectiveness - In order to maintain your motivation it is important that you find a way to measure how effective you are in moving towards your goals. For example, if you join a group to lose weight, the requirements of diet and exercise should be so clear that you'll easily be able to measure whether or not you are losing weight. For this reason it is important that you know where you started from and that's why repeated use of the *Life Situation Assessment* and the associated *Log* will help you measure your progress. Once you are able to identify behaviours related to each of your chosen goals it will be easy for you to measure your progress.

Being able to measure your successes will also help to reinforce and motivate you further.

(A.R.T.) Goals should be achievable and realistic - Make your goals **realistic** and **achievable**. Identify the first step towards the goal and how this might be achieved. If you want to work on more than one area in your life, tackle the areas in order of perceived importance. Identify strategies which you may have used in the past to solve similar problems. Can these be used again?

So if you want to changes in your physical health, work, social life, or relationship then you might want to state your goals like this:

Physical: *"I will run for 20 mins three times per week to improve my physical health."*

Work: *"I will apply for one to three jobs per week."*

Social: *"I will join a club this week and say hello to 3 people."*

Relationship: *"I will buy a gift for my partner this week to show them how much I care for them."*

As you can see these goal statements are, in most cases, **achievable** and **realistic**. They also are **time specific** and so meet all the requirements of S.M.A.R.T. approach to goals. They are positive, personal and meet the need for good health, work, or relationships.

In keeping with the 'Life Situation Assessment' discussed earlier you might want to make your goals **S.M.A.R.T.E.R.** In SMARTER goals the **E** relates to your *emotions,* your *emotional state.* If you care too little about your chosen goal then you are unlikely to achieve it. If you care too much then this may also cause you problems because, as mentioned earlier, strong emotions affect your ability to make effective decisions. Pursuing a goal in the wrong emotional state will, inevitably, be difficult and you may well lose your motivation or develop an obsession. So, make sure you care enough, but not too much, about your chosen goal and its benefits.

E can also stand for the ecology of your chosen goal. Every decision you make and every goal you choose will have an impact on you and the people around you. So, you might want to take a few moments to ask yourself what potential impact your chosen goal will have on your friends, your family, you career, your social life, your financial situation and your health. In short what effect will achieving this goal have on your life and those around you. By going through this process you will give yourself the opportunity to prepare for possible problems that you may encounter in the future. Having given these problems thought at this stage means you will be far better equipped to manage them effectively should they arise. In the words of a well known proverb: *"Forewarned is forearmed."* Dr Michael Yapko believes that 'foresight' is one of the most essential skills to develop. With enough foresight you will be in a position to avoid many pitfalls that may lie ahead as you work towards meeting your desired goal(s).

In **SMARTER** goals the **R** refers to making sure that you have a wide *range* strategies or approaches that will help you reach your goal. Remember that if you are struggling to reach a goal it may be that there is a weakness in your strategy. If this is the case then having a *range* of strategies will increase your chances of success.

As you look over your chosen goal or goals take a few moments to remind yourself of parts 4 and 5 of the change process:

4. Consider the **costs of choosing different solutions**. "If I .... then I'll have to .... Keep in mind the various possibilities because there is no cost-free or painless way of dealing with a problem or making a change.

5. If you have reached the time when the problem situation is now seen for what it is, it is impossible to retreat and so **a more**

serious weighing of choices takes place. Be aware of the costs of changing versus the costs of leaving things as they are. Accept the dialogue that may go on in your mind between steps 4 and 5.

Costs of choosing different solutions - It is very important that you take the time to consider the costs of your chosen solutions. Think of, and write down, any obstacles that might prevent you achieving your goals. If you fail to do this then when you meet any obstacles you could lose motivation and this will discourage you from pursuing your chosen goals.

Accessing resources - Having listed the **costs** of your chosen solution you now need to feel able to take on the large task of making the necessary changes in their life. You may be lacking self-confidence or you may feel that you do not possess the necessary skills to be able to achieve your goals.

You need to do something straight away to increase your confidence in your abilities. A quick way to achieve this is to look over your life and to make an 'inventory' of your successes and achievements you have already have in your life. This will focus you on the fact that you have already taken on many challenges and succeeded and made changes. So you could ask yourself *"What do I have going for me?"* and list everything you think might help you achieve the goal of, for example, creating a more interesting interpersonal life. The list might include:

> *I'm a caring person. I care about others and would like to be helpful when I can. I'm organised and self-disciplined.*
>
> *I'm an intelligent human being. I usually have a good idea of what to do in social situations, even though sometimes I'm a little aloof.*
>
> *Some people at work and the neighbours have already shown an interest in me, although I've been afraid to encourage them.*
>
> *I'm very lonely right now so my motivation to change is high.*
>
> *I live in a large city where there are all sorts of places I could meet and get to know people.*

You can now continue the list and add any other resources that you can think of. The more complete the list the better but don't feel you have to go on and on. The main purpose is to *act*, not just make a list of all your resources.

The benefit of making this list is it that will help you to realise that you have a lot of resources available and also provide you with 'tools' which you can use to help you achieve your chosen goals. The materials in this book will also provide you with other 'tools' you can use to help you achieve your goals.

Deciding a strategy for change - The next area you need to look at is your strategy. Having identified goals you now need to take a more detailed look at how. This could be a change in your behaviour. For example, becoming more physically active, mixing socially or practising social skills. With regards to couples they often need some activity that will make them feel good about each other, because, often, they have stopped doing things that they used to do together with pleasure. When partners feel good again in each other's company, they are always more willing to make changes. It is therefore important to structure joint activities such as going for walks, to the cinema, or anything that they previously enjoyed, where they are giving each other positive attention.

What you learn through reading this book and doing the exercises can have powerful effects on you and your life. Learning about how values, beliefs and relaxation skills can affect your behaviour and state of mind can often lead to changes in your life. Identifying boundaries and managing the roles in your life more effectively will also have a great impact on your life. Learning when and how to say 'no' to people is just one example of establishing your boundaries.

However difficult your life circumstances, there have been others who have dealt with something similar without generating for themselves additional psychological suffering. Additional psychological suffering is very often caused by a misuse of imagination, black and white thinking, catastrophic thinking, excessive focusing on the negative and so on. The tool of the cognitive mind can be used highly effectively, to help you to think in a more realistic way, learning how to de-catastrophise your thinking and become aware of unhelpful black and white thinking which cannot bear uncertainty.

Some people may see their partner smiling and laughing with members of the opposite sex and assume the worst, but the simple strategy of challenging faulty thinking can be used to overcome this problem. So, when they see their partner smiling and laughing with someone else then challenge this instant assumption that they are flirting and remind themselves that it is more likely they are just engaging in normal social chitchat.

Implementation - The heart of living effectively is taking action, ridding yourself of destructive behaviour patterns, enhancing current constructive patterns, and implementing new constructive patterns. If your action plan has been carefully thought out (that is, if it is systematic and involves no step that is too complicated), you will move the process of change step by step. If you try to do too much too soon you may well feel overwhelmed, lose heart and may well abandon your efforts.

Making changes in your life may well uncover new problems or further dimensions of problems. For instance, a man improves his relationship with his wife but begins to have trouble with his son. When you make changes in your life and begin to act differently it is highly likely that there will be a reaction from your environment in unexpected ways. When this happens it may be necessary to modify your action programme

Relapse or 'Falling Back' - Once you have begun to take action you need to maintain your progress and also be aware of **relapse** and **falling back**. Always remember that **relapse** or **falling back** into a previous undesired behaviour is not failure. It is merely feedback and gives you the opportunity to re-examine your strategy. Take the time you need to do this and make any necessary changes to your action plan.

Success Patterning - A useful method you can use to help you achieve your goals is known as "Success Patterning" and this is described in detail in the Resources Section.

The goals setting process has been described in some detail above but before leaving this topic remember that goal setting is only part of the process. A goal gives you something to aim for. When pursuing any goal it is also essential that you consider *how* you will achieve the goal and *why* you wish to achieve that goal. There is little point working 18 hours a day, and damage your health to become a millionaire and ignoring your family and friends. You may well achieve your 'goal' of becoming a millionaire but you may also lose your family and friends along the way.

You've now reached the end of the goals section. Now might be a useful time to do the following exercise as it will give you the opportunity to reflect on the goals you have chosen, the kind of life you'd like to create and the kind of life you'd like to live.

The Rocking Chair

Purpose: To create some future-oriented imagery that can motivate your taking positive action now.

Imagine yourself at some time in the future when you have retired and are sitting in your 'rocking chair' and re-telling your life to a young child.

Review the things in your life of which you are most proud. What would you describe as your greatest sources of pride? Which of these required great effort and careful planning?

Next consider what you would like other people to say about you and your life? Someone from your family, secondly a friend, thirdly a professional colleague.

What would you like each of these people to say about your life? What kind of husband, wife, mother, father or friend would you like their words to reflect? What kind of friend? What kind of working associate?

What character would you like them to have seen in you? What contributions, what achievements, would you want them to remember?

Next, review your life in terms of potential regrets. What would you most regret not having done? What reasons or excuses would you offer for not having done it?

Now, think twice before you decide that it's too late to do the things you would regret not having done. That rocking chair is many, many years away.

THE OBSERVING SELF

"Human beings are a race that sleeps and awakens, but does not fully awaken. Because half-awake is sufficient for the tasks we customarily do."

Deikman

Deikman[1] In his book **"The Observing Self"** suggests we spend most of our time in 'trance' or a state of 'self-hypnosis' and this allows us to look upon reality in a particular way. In order to break these trance states it is necessary to develop the observing self.

Deikman identifies four selves. These are; *The Thinking Self, The Emotional Self, The Functional Self* and finally *The Observing Self.*

The *'Thinking Self'* is concerned with planning, solving problems, worrying, imagining. It is our logical and rational 'self'.

The *'Emotional Self'* involves emotions like anxiety, joy, anger and desire. At times this aspect of ourselves might seem like the most dominant part of ourselves for nothing seems to be more completely our self than our emotions.

The *'The Functional Self'* is that part of our self which involves the experience of our functional capacity. I know that I do things: I am aware of my acting, my capacity to affect the world around me. My body is the main part of the functional self.

The *'Observing self'* is the state of being aware of awareness itself. When in this state we have the potential to look in many directions, and to choose to focus our attention in a variety of ways. On one level, by developing our ability to relax we can lower the level of emotional arousal and this allows people to function without excessive emotional interference, enabling us to look at a situation more constructively. The observing self 'view' on a situation offers an alternative to the emotional 'view'.

The observing self gives us the ability to delay, and even break up emotional and thought responses, and asks, *"Look, is this the appropriate way to go? What other possibilities are there? What might be the consequences if*

I take a certain course of action?" That is what the observing self enables us to do. When we keep calm and engage it we can look at, for instance, a traumatic memory and say: *"Yes, that was a dangerous moment at that time, but that was then, in the past, which is not now."*

The observing self works best when a person is in a relaxed state of low emotional arousal.

We are more than our experiences. No matter what failures we have, no matter what unpleasant life circumstances a person may be trapped in, we are always more than the content of our life. The observing self gives a person the opportunity to 'stand back' and take a look at themselves, others and their situation. From this position it is easier to make decisions and live life more effectively.

Accessing the observing self

Stage 1: Do something that encourages relaxation. This does not necessarily mean doing a relaxation exercise. To become aware and see themselves more objectively, people just need to be fairly calm so that they are not 'hijacked' by emotions.

Stage 2: Consider the problem/symptom as though it were *outside* of yourself: or do something that has the same effect.

Questions and actions that may help

Examples of questions that do this:

"What does this habit do to you ?"

"When do you sense that anger is coming?"

"How does stress/anxiety fool me into thinking in such black and white terms?"

"What name shall we give this anger (or other problem) ?"

All of these questions contain the presupposition that the person is not the problem. The problem is outside the person.

Statements that do the same thing:

"I'm not Parkinson's disease / cancer / multiple sclerosis (etc.)."

"Panic attacks are just the 'fight or flight' response going off inappropriately, actually I'm fine."

Behavioural example

Many people are so self absorbed that they hardly look at you when talking about their miseries. If they say some outrageously unrealistic thing like, *"I never laugh,"* or *"everybody hates me,"* look in the mirror and ask yourself, *"I never laugh?"* *"everybody hates me."* If you ask the question to yourself in such a way you may well realise that it's not true and .... begin to smile. This is because you are forcing yourself out of trance and into your observing self.

Imaginative example

Using visualisation encourages you to view the problem as outside yourself. For example, depression can be seen as a huge black cloud hovering above and then be blown into the distance until it is tiny. Or consider doing the exercise below:

Right Proportions

Picture in detail the room in which you are sitting, as well as everything around you. Now, in your imagination, move up and away from the room and form a clear picture of the building that contains it.

See the building getting smaller as you rise higher and higher. From above, the whole area in which you live lies below you: houses, streets, trees, parks, high rise buildings. People and cars are just barely visible in the streets. Think how each person is the centre of their own world, with their own thoughts and hopes, their own problems and projects. Watch them all moving around, living their own lives. Imagine them in their homes too.

Continue your ascent. Your field of view expands, enabling you to see other towns in the area, green fields, mountains and lakes.

As you rise higher and higher, you can glimpse oceans and other countries as well as banks of clouds.

Now you have the whole planet Earth before you, blue and white, slowly rotating in empty space. From this immense height you can no longer see people or even guess their existence; but you can think of them, six billion people, each one living on that same planet, breathing the same air. Six billion hearts of people of many different races are beating down there. Think about this for a while, as you continue to visualise the planet Earth.

Now, as you move away from it, you see the Earth becoming smaller and smaller. Other planets enter your field of view: bright Venus, red Mars, massive Jupiter – in fact the whole solar system.

The Earth has now vanished, the sun is but a tiny point of light among innumerable stars, and you have lost all trace of it. Billions of stars are all around you, below, above, on all sides. There is no more 'down' no more 'up.'

All these billions of stars constitute but one galaxy in the universe. It is one among an unknown number of other galaxies reaching out in every direction to infinity.

At this point, think of the infinity of time. Here there is no 'tomorrow' and no 'yesterday', no haste, no pressure. Everything is scintillating peace and wonder.

When you feel inclined to do so, open your eyes again and bring back with you this sense of expansion.

Every exercise in this book is designed to help you to raise your awareness and develop your 'observing self'. The exercises give you the opportunity to take a step back and look at many aspects of your life that affect your ability to live effectively. The development of awareness and the observing self are of the utmost importance if you want to learn the 'art of living' and I hope you will give all the exercises in this book the time required so that you are in a position to live your life in a way you would like to live it, to do the things you would like to do and, most importantly, to be the kind of person you would like to be.

THINGS NOT TO DO

(Adapted from the work of Michael Yapko)

Throughout this book the emphasis has been to provide you with 'tools' you can actively use to help yourself. Now though I want to offer a brief list of things **not to do** if you are attempting to change aspects of your life.

Do Not Dwell On The Past

The past is over, and history can't be changed. Change is not about bad choices in the past, it's about how you interpreted those choices and the skills you didn't have at the time for dealing with them. What matters now is what happens tomorrow and in the future. Make changes *now* to overcome the teachings of your past that were hurtful, wrong or ineffective. Focusing on the past does *not* necessarily teach you new skills, it can simply rehash old stuff. Look forward, because tomorrow hasn't happened yet, and the possibilities are wondrous.

Do Not Compare Yourself To Others

You are unique as an individual. By making comparisons to others you can distract yourself from the more immediate task at hand, which is identifying the specific experiences you need to have, and the skills you need to learn in order to make the changes in *your* life. There will *always* be people who are a little better and a little worse than you: your most important task is developing yourself to the fullest extent possible. You are you, and there isn't another you anywhere – so be the best you that you can possibly be.

Do Not Create And Dwell On Negative Possibilities

While it can be good to anticipate potential snags in your plans, the larger picture should be one of what you can do what is useful, not the negatives to be avoided. Whoever said, "obstacles are what you see when you take your eye off the goal" definitely had the right idea. Your goals help define your character, the purpose of your life, and they fuel the optimism of what the "good life" can be for you. Aim for the target.

Do Not Leave Important Things Unsaid Or Undefined

For all the things that directly affect your feelings about yourself –
your relationships, your health, your job – these are things that should
be well defined and skillfully managed. Keep yourself focused on how
to do things skillfully. If you don't know *how* to do something, learn
it. *Don't* give up!

Do Not Ignore Your Own Needs

Change can be very difficult if you invest more heavily in others
or in external situations. It is essential that you learn to **balance** your
needs against the needs of others to make healthy changes. Other
people matter, but you are in no position to make effective changes if
you don't take good care of yourself first.

Do Not Ignore Reality In Order To Blindly Follow Your Own Wishes And Desires

To focus on your own goals and wishes to the exclusion of
understanding the realities of the environment in which you live
means that you will respond ineffectively to the world around you.
Remember, you can't always trust your feelings. Your feelings can
deceive you, so make 'reality testing' a habit. Watch for evidence, listen
carefully to things people say (and don't say) and set your feelings
and reactions aside until you're clear about what's going on. A little
'impulse control' can go a long way.

Do Not Give Up

To expend effort and fail, in whatever way failure might be defined,
is painful. The things you want to do are most likely possible. Success
or failure comes as a result of the strategy you follow to produce an
outcome. If you try to do something and fail, don't give up and don't
just do the same thing harder. *Do something else!* If you see other people
who can do it, that means it can be done. If you do not know what to
do, find someone who can show you how. *If you fail, it is not a reflection
of your capability as much as it is a statement of how you went about doing it.*
It is vitally important that you continue to expend effort and to do so

intelligently, in a focused way. When you do not know what to do, get help; that is a far more effective response than giving up and assuming you can't succeed. No one succeeds in all things they attempt to do. As Thomas Edison said, "Genius is about 5 percent inspiration, and 95 percent perspiration."

Do Not Leave Time Unstructured

Time can be your greatest ally, depending on how you use it. Structure your daily experiences to bring out your best. If you feel good when you are out in nature, for example, then get out there as much as you can. Build your schedule to include a balance of work with play, time with others with time alone, physical rest with physical exertion, and so forth. Schedule yourself for good times.

Do Not Stop Working To Improve Yourself

You now know what is involved in making changes in your life. It is a good idea to continually monitor yourself, your thoughts, your feelings, your relationships, your values, your habits. Always remember the quest for self-improvement is never ending. You may never be perfect, but you can be *really good*.

THINGS TO DO

"People ask. " What can I actually do?" The answer is as simple as it is disconcerting: we can, each of us, work to put our own inner house in order. The answers are in 'traditional wisdom', not technology."

E.F. Schumacher

All of the ideas and techniques presented in this book have given you many different 'tools' that you can use to make changes in your life. This is not meant to be a book you read once, as if it were a novel. Instead, I hope you will continually use the exercises and ideas to keep developing new understandings and competencies, and new ways to enhance all the good things you already are.

Since so much about this book is discussing what to do, my final pieces of advice are quite brief and to the point:

1.   Appreciate that stressful things happen in *every life*, and change happens in *every* life, not just yours. Managing change ineffectively can lead to many stresses. *Managing stress effectively, thinking ahead, being able to relax, and stepping outside the immediacy of the situation* are all important skills for maintaining your balance and managing changes in your life.

2.   Developing *effective change-management* skills is vital to managing your life effectively. Dealing with what *is* instead of fantasising about how things should or can be is the necessary starting place. Having dreams and goals is great, but reality is the starting place to build the bridge between 'here' and 'there.'

3.   A great deal of importance has been placed on *self-awareness*, particularly in the areas of your personal needs, values and beliefs. The importance of personal integrity – your behaving in a way that is consistent with your needs and values, and respectful of others as well – cannot be overstated. I want you to watch yourself liking what you see as you move through life. Living a life with integrity is the foundation of good *self-esteem*.

4.   The need to *make changes in your life around factors within your control whenever possible* is particularly important. Be especially careful

about whom you get attached to or dependent on. The tendency to get victimised easily or assume too much control means any change you invest yourself in is potentially hazardous.

You can't control other people, of course, but you can choose carefully whom you bring into your life. Bring in people who enhance you, who bring out the parts in you that you really like, such as your sensitivity, your humour, your playfulness and affection. Treat yourself as if you deserve good people in your life who can appreciate you. Why? Because you deserve good people in your life who can appreciate you.

ADDITIONAL RESOURCES

Seeking Help

When making changes in life many people are able to manage the process themselves. However, there may be occasions when you feel you need some 'professional' help with the process. If you decide to seek help then bear the following in mind. There is no shortage of people in the coaching, counselling and the personal development world who will be more than willing to help you. Some may say there is a major difference between coaching and counselling and that coaching focuses on the future and counselling on the past. This is quite simply misleading and largely wrong. There are some schools of counselling that focus on the past and are non-directive. There are many others that focus on the present and future.

When looking for help take some time to do some research about anyone you are considering. Find out what their background and experience is, what their qualifications are, where they trained and what their training covered, whether or not they are insured. Also you might ask for an initial meeting to find out if their approach is the right approach for you. If the person is reluctant or unwilling to answer your questions then you might want to consider whether or not they are the right person for you.

Also consider the guidelines given below.

An effective coach, counsellor, teacher or psychotherapist:

√ helps immediately with anxiety problems including stress or fear related symptoms.

√ understands emotional and psychological difficulties and how to manage them.

√ is prepared to give information and advice as needed.

√ will not use jargon or 'psychobabble' or tell you that the process has to be 'painful'.

√ will not dwell unduly on the past.

148

√ will be supportive when difficult feelings emerge, but will not encourage people to get emotional beyond the normal need to 'let go' of any bottled up feelings.

√ may assist you to develop your self-management, people skills and behavioural skills so that you are better equipped to manage all areas in your life including the ability to give and receive affection, be effective at work, develop friendships, enjoy life, have successful relationships and connect to the wider community.

√ will help you to become aware of the resources, skills and abilities you possess, develop new ones and draw on these as required.

√ will be considerate of the effects of coaching / counselling on the people close to you and may teach you how to relax deeply.

√ will help you think about your problems in new and more constructive ways.

√ uses a wide range of techniques as appropriate and may ask you to do things between sessions , will take as few sessions as possible.

√ will increase your self-confidence and independence.

Life Situation Assessment

Use a scoring system from 1 to 10 (10 being the optimum score), that reflects your personal fulfilment, contentment, happiness and overall satisfaction with your present situation. It also gives you an indicator as to how well these general needs are being met at the present time. Address each area briefly and select a score based on your initial feelings.

	Low									High
• Health – Quality of Food	1	2	3	4	5	6	7	8	9	10
Amount of Food	1	2	3	4	5	6	7	8	9	10
Amount of Exercise	1	2	3	4	5	6	7	8	9	10
• Personal Growth	1	2	3	4	5	6	7	8	9	10
• Work/Career	1	2	3	4	5	6	7	8	9	10
• Financial	1	2	3	4	5	6	7	8	9	10
• Personal Relationships	1	2	3	4	5	6	7	8	9	10
• Family/extended family	1	2	3	4	5	6	7	8	9	10
• Friends/social life	1	2	3	4	5	6	7	8	9	10
• Physical environment	1	2	3	4	5	6	7	8	9	10
• Fun and Recreation	1	2	3	4	5	6	7	8	9	10

Low Mood   High Mood

• How would you describe your emotional state?

Remember to review your scores on a regular basis.

It is very important to remember this is not about "beating yourself up" it's about helping you to get an idea of areas you might want to do some work on.

If, after a few weeks of completing the survey, your scores are consistently low in one area this might well indicate that you need to address this area and do something to meet the need that has not been met.

With regards to your emotional state. If you remain in a low or high mood for a long period of time then you need to do something to change your mood as this may be a warning sign that you are particularly stressed at this time.

LIFE SITUATION ASSESSMENT – LOG SHEET

Use a scoring system from 1 to 10, (10 being the optimum score), that reflects your personal fulfilment, contentment, happiness and overall satisfaction with your present situation. It also gives you an indicator as to how well these general needs are being met at the present time. Address each area briefly and select a score based on your initial feelings.

Remember to review your scores on a regular basis.

Date							
Score 1 - 10							
Health - Quality of Food							
Amount of Food							
Amount of Exercise							
Personal Growth							
Work/Career							
Financial							
Personal Relationships							
Family/extended family							
Friends/social life							
Physical environment							
Fun and Recreation							
Mood / Emotional State (High/ OK/Low)							

Remember this is not about "beating yourself up" it's about helping you to get an idea of areas you might want to do some work on.

If, after a few weeks of completing the survey, your scores are consistently low in one area this might well indicate that you need to address this area and do something to meet the need that has not been met.

With regards to your emotional state. If you remain in a low or high mood high for a long period of time then you need to do something change your mood as this may be a warning sign that you are particularly stressed at this time.

Complaint, Criticism, Or Contempt?

To review the all-important difference between complaints, criticism, and contempt, take this quick quiz. For each statement, circle whether you think it is a sign of complaint, criticism, or contempt.

1. "I am upset that you didn't pay the gas bill."
Complaint Criticism Contempt

2. "How can I ever trust you?"
Complaint Criticism Contempt

3. "You are totally irresponsible."
Complaint Criticism Contempt

4. "You stupid jerk!"
Complaint Criticism Contempt

5. "I should have known you'd pull something like that."
Complaint Criticism Contempt

6. "You are just terrible with the kids."
Complaint Criticism Contempt

7. "When we don't go out together I feel like you take me for granted."
Complaint Criticism Contempt

8. "I wish that you'd touch me more and be more affectionate"
Complaint Criticism Contempt

9. "Don't interrupt!"
Complaint Criticism Contempt

10. "You just never care about my feelings."
Complaint Criticism Contempt

11. "Leave it to you and you screw up the vacation plans!"
Complaint Criticism Contempt

12. "Whose fault is it then?"
Complaint Criticism Contempt

13. "Don't tell me you didn't know any better."
Complaint Criticism Contempt

14. "I'm sick to death of your behaviour."
Complaint Criticism Contempt

15. "Have you got an attitude problem?"
Complaint Criticism Contempt

16. "When you don't listen to me I feel unimportant."
Complaint Criticism Contempt

17. "I'm upset you didn't clean up the dishes last night."
Complaint Criticism Contempt

18. "You're just like your mother!"
Complaint Criticism Contempt

19. "How can you hurt me like this?"

Complaint Criticism Contempt

ANSWER KEY

1. Complaint
2. Criticism
3. Contempt
4. Contempt
5. Contempt
6. Criticism
7. Complaint
8. Complaint
9. Complaint
10. Criticism

11. Contempt
12. Criticism
13. Criticism
14. Criticism
15. Criticism
16. Complaint
17. Complaint
18. Contempt
19. Criticism

Give yourself one point for each correct answer. If you score below 16 points you probably need more clarification to know the differences between the "Three C's. "

- A **complaint** is *specific,* limited to one situation. It states how you feel. ("I am upset because you didn't take out the rubbish tonight.")

- A **criticism** tends to be global and *includes blaming* your partner. You'll often find the word *always* or *never* in a criticism. {"You never take out the garbage. Now it's overflowed and that's your fault. I can't ever rely on you;")

- **Contempt** adds insult to the criticism. It is verbal character assassination in which you accuse your spouse of stupidity, incompetence, etc. ("You idiot, why can't you ever remember to take out the garbage?")

If you understand how a complaint differs from criticism or contempt but still have difficulty controlling yourself from being negative during an argument, keep the following general guidelines in mind:

- Remove the blame from your comments.

- Don't criticise the other person's personality.

- Don't insult, mock, or use sarcasm.

- Be direct.

- Stick with one situation.
- Don't try to analyse the other person's personality.
- Don't mind-read.
- Say how you feel

Most of all, try to be as specific as possible when you complain. The more concrete your grievance, the more you'll improve the other persons understanding of why you're upset. Think of your complaint as a set of directions. We all know how easy it is to follow instructions that are clear and explicit. If someone says, "Go two miles and turn right at the gas station with the big plastic dinosaur on top," you know exactly where to go. But if the same person were to simply wave his arms to the right, look to the left, and say soothingly, "It's just down there a piece. Can't miss it," you'd be headed for nowhere. In much the same way, a specific complaint lets the other person know exactly where you are, while vague complaints can be misinterpreted and get you off track.

(This questionnaire can be found in "Why Marriages Succeed and Fail and How to Make Yours Last" by John Gottman)

Criticism & Complaint Part II

A good way to keep a complaint specific is to couch it in what is known as an "X, Y, Z" statement. Think of this approach as a kind of game in which you fill in the blanks with your particular gripe in mind:

"When you did (or didn't do) **X** in situation **Y**, I felt **Z**."

Example: "When you didn't call to tell me you were going to be late (X) for our dinner appointment (Y), I felt frustrated (Z)." Using this X, Y, Z formula will help you avoid insults and character assassination. It allows you to simply state how the other person's behaviour affects your feelings and, in turn your response.

Let's say you're upset about the finances. It's more constructive to say, "When you bounced several checks (X) and the bank called (Y), I, felt embarrassed and angry (Z)," rather than, "You are incredibly irresponsible for bouncing a cheque, I'm constantly having to pick up after your mistakes and fix everything you screw up."

Another example of a specific complaint: "I felt so left out when you spent all night at your sister's house." (You can change the order of the X, Y, and Z to fit the way you naturally talk.) This is far more helpful to the other person than saying, "You're never home at night." Although the latter may be what first comes to your mind, it's really just an exercise in verbal fog-and it's likely to draw a defensive response from the other person.

It's especially common for couples to be non-specific when talking about sexual issues, a discussion that is by its nature delicate and sensitive and therefore prone to defensiveness. "I'm just not very satisfied with sex" or "you could be a better lover" is pretty devastating news and pretty perplexing since it leaves your partner not knowing where or how to respond-except with hurt feelings.

Compare that with, "When you touch me here before we've cuddled for a while it's hard for me to relax," or, "when you want to have sex right when I get home from work it makes me feel dehumanised." (Incidentally, sex talks go even better if you emphasise what you *do* enjoy rather than what you don't: "I really like it when you touch me here," "it's so much fun when we make time to take a bath together,"etc.)

Two other manners of speaking that can trigger a defensive response in another person are a belligerent and domineering style. Domineering speech lets the other person know you want him or her to respond only as you see fit *"When I want your opinion I'll give it to you."* Whether your tone is threatening or patronising, your message is the same: you've got the floor and you're not giving it up. Certainly not to the other person. You may repeat yourself simply to maintain your "rights" as speaker. Domineering speech may be very slow and deliberate, indicating that you're adamant about your point of view and nothing is going to change it. *Or* your tone may be condescending, indicating that the other person is a simple child who needs to be shown the right way.

Belligerent talk lets the other person know you're really ready to fight. At the very least, you want to get a rise out of him or her. Phrases like, "Do you have an attitude problem or what?" "What is it *now?" Just trying to get on my nerves, is that it?" "What have you got to say for yourself? "What's your complaint? Speak up,"* are signs of this bullying.

If you recognise yourself in the description of belligerent or domineering speaking (or if another person recognises you), you must work especially hard *not* to talk this way during arguments. No matter what justifications you may believe you have for these responses, the reality is that you will never be able to communicate effectively if you subject another person to blatant or veiled threats.

Training yourself to speak to another person in a way that doesn't trigger a negative response will greatly cut down on the other person's defensiveness, which can only improve the communication between you. But it isn't enough. After all, at times when you'll be on the receiving end of a destructive, negative statement or look from another person. What do you do then? Most people reflexively become defensive in an attempt to ward off the attack. But as I'm sure you know by now, such phrases usually have the opposite effect, dragging you both further into a quagmire of accusations and hurt feelings.

When you're responding to a less-than-perfect comment from another person it's up to you to extricate both of you from a nasty, counter productive confrontation. To do so, you need to avoid the defensive responses below.

- Denying responsibility for a problem
- Using phrases like "yes, but. .,"
- Whining
- Reacting to negative mind-reading
- Cross-complaining
- Using the "rubber man" or "rubberwoman" ploy
- Falling back on the repeating yourself syndrome

- Making excuses

Instead try to respond in a way that lets the other person know you're considering his or her perspective, even if you don't agree with it.

Validation

Letting another person know in so many little ways that you understand him or her is one of the most powerful tools for healing any relationship. It is an antidote to criticism, contempt, and defensiveness. Instead of attacking or ignoring the other person's point of view, you try to see the problem from their perspective, and show that you think that viewpoint may have some validity.

Validation is especially important for men who tend to respond to their wives' upset by becoming hyper rational. Rather than acknowledge the emotional content of their wife's words, they try to offer practical solutions to the problem being described. This can be quite well meaning, but it often misses the mark. If your wife is being extremely emotional she probably isn't interested in hearing advice. She mostly needs to know that you understand what she's *feeling*.

Validation is simply putting yourself in the other person's shoes and imagining his or her emotional state. It is then a simple matter to let them know that you understand those feelings and consider them valid, even if you don't share them, Validation is an amazingly effective technique. It's as if you opened the door to welcome the other person. When the other person feels validated; he or she will feel much more comfortable confiding in you, and much more open to hearing your perspective as well.

Validation is a real art and has many gradations. At the top of the scale is true empathy and understanding, This entails actually feeling a bit of what the other person is experiencing and being able to see the world through their eyes; expressing this deep empathy will show that you not only understand the other person's view of the world but also his or her sense of self. Few things make a person feel more loved and valued, There are some specific ways you can add a high level of validation to your talks.

Take Responsibility. If someone close to you says he/she gets upset when you don't call to let them know you'll be late for a meeting, try answering with, "Gee, I really made you angry, didn't 1?"You are acknowledging that your actions might have provoked the other person's response.

Apologize. Similarly, a straight-out apology is a very strong form of validation because it lets the other person know you consider his or her grievance valid and worth respecting. To apologise you don't have to always say, "I'm sorry." You can simply say, "I see what you mean. I was wrong." Everyone is wrong from time to time. However, admitting this in an argument can have very powerful results.

Compliment. Honestly praising another person for handling a situation well will go a long way. Especially when there is tension between you, reminding the other person (and yourself) that you really admire him or her is likely to have a powerful, positive effect on the rest of your conversation.

Doing the Minimum. At first, you may not be able to muster these high forms of validation. Fortunately, even a relatively minor type of validation, simply listening to and acknowledging the other person's point of view even if you don't share it, can work wonders, This type of validation can be as straightforward as saying, "Yes, I know that upsets you," when someone says they are   concerned about your work.. Be careful, however, not to end the sentence by harping on the fact that you don't agree. Do this and you'll cancel out the validation. Right now, your job isn't to argue for your point but to let the other person know you understand his or hers.

Learning How To Relax
7:11 Breathing
Progressive Muscle relaxation

Guided Imagery session
Exercise
Listening to music

Overlearning-Try And Try Again

When you've had one successful "fight" using these techniques you may think you've mastered the strategies. I'm afraid there's more work involved. In fact, the worst thing you could do is to do the exercises once and never look at them again. It's not enough to have an intellectual understanding of "fighting smart." These techniques have to be practised *often*. So often, in fact, that they become almost automatic. This is true when you learn any new skill. You didn't just sail out of the driveway the first time you learned to drive; you didn't lob the ball over the net the first time you played tennis; no doubt your first chocolate souffle did not rise evenly. So practise, practise, practise!

(Adapted from: "Why Marriages Succeed and Fail and How to Make Yours Last" by John Gottman)

Success Patterning - 3 Weeks Practise minimum

Another process that can help you achieve your desired goal and develop confidence is to use a process known as **Success Patterning.** The aim of this process is that it becomes a natural part of how we go about things. Regular use will create an invisible part of your natural thought processes.

Success Statement

When considering a situation you need to focus on what you want in a situation and not what you don't want.

"When I give my presentation next week I'd like to feel calm, energetic and focused. To deliver my speech with energy and passion and to welcome any questions my audience has."

Success and confidence is based on specific situations and it is not a good idea to make general statement as its not specific and it's not realistic. Success statements have to be specific and realistic.

Compare the above statement with – *"I want to be calm, focused and relaxed"* which is non specific.

Emotional Example

The next part of the process is to bring back to your mind the feeling you want to experience. You can do this by thinking of a time, previously or any time, that you felt the way that you wish to feel again.

Mental Rehearsal

We can now bring in the final part which is the **rapid rehearsal**. In this part you can imagine yourself giving the presentation with the feeling you wish to evoke. By going through this process you are more likely to feel the way you want to feel in a situation and have a more successful outcome.

It is better to practise this process when you are feeling good and relaxed. For example in the bath or just after some exercise.

Once this process becomes habit you will start to do success patterning without thinking. Once you have your statements you will not have to do it again and you will have a collection of statements that you can use in all situations.

The Autonomic Nervous System

The autonomic system has a wide range of powerful effects on the on the mind/body system. It is hoped that by reading what follows the importance of the autonomic nervous in maintaining or regaining 'balance' in the mind/body system will be better understood. This in turn will help you to understand the importance of **stimulating the relaxation response** in yourself.

The autonomic nervous system consists of two parts. The **sympathetic** and the **parasympathetic.** The actions of the two systems are carefully integrated to help maintain homeostasis.

The parasympathetic division is primarily concerned with activities that restore and conserve body energy. It is a rest-repose system. Under normal body conditions, for instance, parasympathetic impulses to the digestive glands and the smooth muscle of the digestive system dominate over sympathetic impulses. Thus, energy-supplying food can be digested and absorbed by the body.

The sympathetic division, in contrast, is primarily concerned with processes involving the expenditure of energy. When the body is in homeostasis, the main function of the sympathetic division is to counteract the parasympathetic effects just enough to carry out normal processes requiring energy. During extreme stress, however, the sympathetic dominates the parasympathetic. When people are confronted with a stress condition, for example, their bodies become alert and they sometimes perform feats of unusual strength. Fear stimulates the sympathetic division.

Activation of the sympathetic division sets into operation a series of physiological responses collectively called the **fight-or-flight response**. It produces the following effects.

1. The pupils of the eyes dilate.
2. The heart rate increases.
3. The blood vessels of the skin and viscera constrict.
4. The remainder of the blood vessels dilate. This causes a faster flow of blood into the dilated blood vessels of skeletal muscles, cardiac muscle, lungs, and brain-organs involved in fighting off danger.

5. Rapid breathing occurs as 'the bronchioles dilate to allow faster movement of air in and out of the lungs.

6. Blood sugar level rises as liver glycogen is converted to glucose to supply the body's additional energy needs.

7. The medulla of the adrenal gland is stimulated to produce epinephrine and norepinephrine, hormones that intensify and prolong the sympathetic effects noted previously.

8. Processes that are not essential for meeting the stress situation are inhibited. For example, muscular movements of the gastrointestinal tract and digestive secretions are slowed down or even stopped.

Control By Higher Centres

The autonomic nervous system is not a separate nervous system. Although little is known about specific centres in the brain that regulate specific autonomic functions, it is known that axons from many parts of the central nervous system are connected to both the sympathetic and the parasympathetic divisions of the autonomic nervous system and thus exert considerable control over it. Autonomic centres in the cerebral cortex are connected to autonomic centres of the thalamus, for example. These, in turn, are connected to the hypothalamus. In this hierarchy of command, the thalamus sorts incoming impulses before they reach the cerebral cortex. The cerebral cortex then turns over control and integration of visceral activation to the hypothalamus. It is at the level of the hypothalamus that the major control and integration of the autonomic nervous system is exerted.

The hypothalamus receives input from areas of the nervous system concerned with emotions, visceral functions, olfaction, gustation, as well as changes in temperature, osmolarity, and levels of various substances in blood. Anatomically, the hypothalamus is connected to both the sympathetic and the parasympathetic divisions of the autonomic nervous system by axons of neurons whose dendrites and cell bodies are in various hypothalamic nuclei. The axons form tracts from the hypothalamus to sympathetic and parasympathetic nuclei in the brain stem and spinal cord through relays in the reticular formation. The posterior and lateral portions of the hypothalamus appear to control the sympathetic division. When these areas are stimulated, there is an increase in visceral activities- an increase in heart rate, a rise in blood pressure due to vasoconstriction of blood vessels, an increase in the rate and depth of respiration, dilation of the pupils, and inhibition of the digestive tract. On the other hand, the anterior and medial portions of the hypothalamus seem to control the parasympathetic division. Stimulation of these areas results in a decrease in heart rate, lowering of blood pressure, constriction of the pupils, and increased motility of the digestive tract.

Control of the autonomic nervous system by the cerebral cortex occurs primarily during emotional stress. In extreme anxiety, which can result from either conscious or subconscious stimulation in the cerebral cortex, the cortex can stimulate the hypothalamus. This, in turn, stimulates the cardiac and vasomotor centres of the medulla, which increases heart rate and blood pressure. If the cortex is stimulated by an extremely unpleasant sight, the stimulation causes vasodilation of blood vessels, a lowering of blood pressure, and fainting.

Evidence of even more direct control of visceral responses is provided by data gathered from studies of bio-feedback and meditation.

Biofeedback

In the simplest terms, biofeedback is a process in which people get constant signals, or feedback, about visceral body functions such as blood pressure, heart rate, and muscle tension. By using special monitoring devices, they can control these visceral functions consciously.

In a study conducted at the Menninger Foundation,★ subjects suffering from migraine headaches received instructions in the use of a monitor that registers the skin temperature of the right index finger. Subjects were also given a typewritten sheet containing to sets of phrases. The first set was designed to help them relax the entire body. The second set was designed to bring about an increased flow of blood in the hands. The subjects practiced raising their skin temperature at home for 5 to 15 minutes a day. When skin temperature increased, the monitor emitted a high-pitched sound. In time, the monitor was abandoned.

Once the subjects learned how to vasodilate their blood vessels, the migraine headaches lessened. Since migraine headaches are believed to involve a distension of blood vessels in the head, the shunting of blood from head to hands relieved the distension and thus the pain.

Other experiments have shown that biofeedback can be applied to childbirth. Women were given monitors hooked up to their fingers and arms to measure electrical conductivity of the skin and skeletal muscle tension. Both conductivity and tension increased with nervousness and made labour difficult. Muscle tension was recorded as a siren like sound that became louder with nervousness. Skin conductivity was recorded as a crackling noise that also increased with nervousness. The monitors kept the women informed of their nervousness. This was the biofeedback. Having pleasant thoughts reduced the sound levels. The reward was less nervousness. The results of the study indicate that the women in a state of reduced nervousness needed less medication during labour, and labour time itself was shortened.

There is no way to determine where biofeedback will lead. Perhaps the outstanding contribution of biofeedback research has been to demonstrate that the autonomic nervous system is not autonomous. Visceral responses can be controlled. Current therapeutic applications of biofeedback include treatment of asthma, Raynaud's disease, hypertension, gastrointestinal disorders, faecal incontinence, anxiety, pain, and neuromuscular rehabilitation.

Meditation

Yoga, which literally means union, is defined as a higher state of consciousness achieved through a fully rested and relaxed body and a fully awake and relaxed mind) One widely practiced technique for achieving higher consciousness is called transcendental meditation (TM). One sits in a comfortable position with the eyes closed and concentrates on a suitable sound or thought.

Research indicates that transcendental meditation can alter physiological responses. Oxygen consumption decreases drastically along with carbon dioxide elimination.. Subjects have experienced a reduction in metabolic rate and blood pressure. Researchers have also observed a decrease in heart rate, an increase in the intensity of alpha brain waves, a sharp decrease in the amount of lactic acid in the blood, and an increase in the skin's electrical resistance. These last four responses are characteristic of a highly relaxed state of mind. Alpha waves are found in the EEGs of almost all individuals in a resting, but awake, state; they disappear during sleep.

These responses have been called an **integrated response** - essentially, a hypo metabolic state due to inactivation of the sympathetic division of the autonomic nervous system. The response is the exact opposite of the fight-or-flight response, which is a hyperactive state of the sympathetic division. The existence of the integrated response suggests that the central nervous system does exert some control over the autonomic nervous system.

Guided Imagery/Hypnosis

For anyone who is familiar with the use of guided imagery/hypnosis they will recognize that many of the effects and benefits gained as a result of biofeedback or meditation can equally be enhanced by the skilful use of guided imagery/hypnosis. It is hoped therefore that you will use these tools wisely and effectively.

★ Much of the discussion of the use of biofeedback for the treatment of migraine headaches is based on information provided by Dr. Joseph D. Sargent of the Menninger Foundation, Topeka, Kansas.

The Autonomic Nervous System

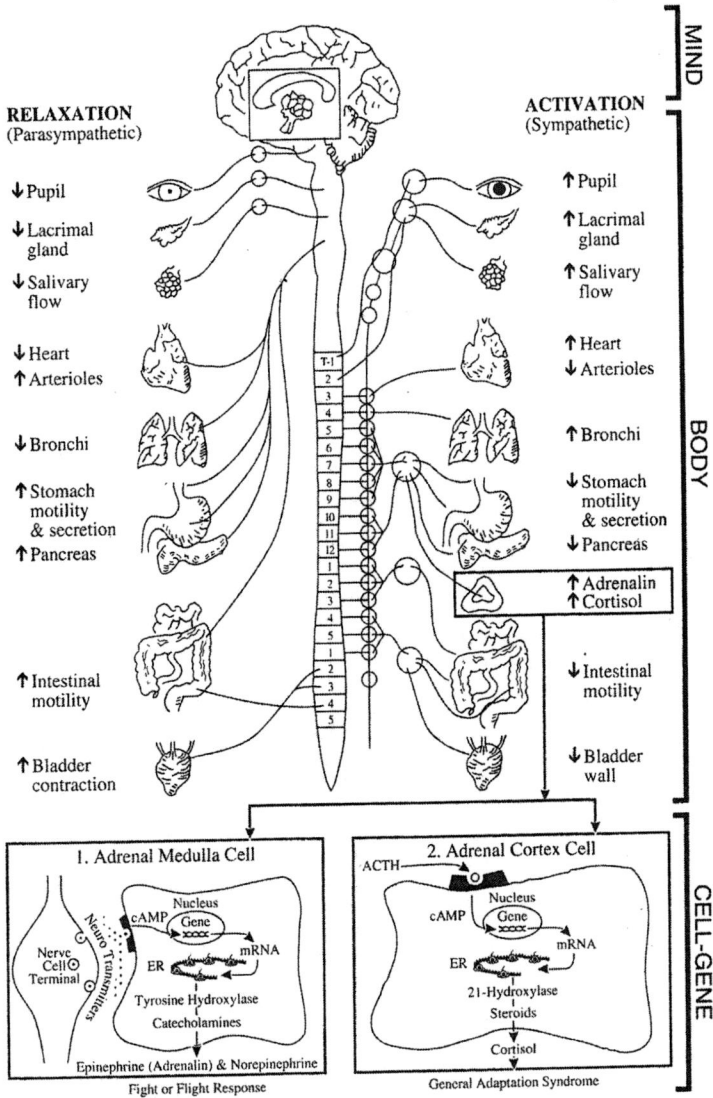

MIND

RELAXATION
(Parasympathetic)

ACTIVATION
(Sympathetic)

↓ Pupil

↑ Pupil

↓ Lacrimal gland

↑ Lacrimal gland

↓ Salivary flow

↑ Salivary flow

↓ Heart
↑ Arterioles

↑ Heart
↓ Arterioles

↓ Bronchi

↑ Bronchi

↑ Stomach motility & secretion
↑ Pancreas

↓ Stomach motility & secretion
↓ Pancreas

↑ Adrenalin
↑ Cortisol

↑ Intestinal motility

↓ Intestinal motility

↑ Bladder contraction

↓ Bladder wall

BODY

T-1
2
3
4
5
6
7
8
9
10
11
12
1
2
3
4
5
1
2
3
4
5

CELL-GENE

1. Adrenal Medulla Cell

Nucleus
cAMP
Gene
XXXX
mRNA
Nerve Cell Terminal
Neuro Transmitters
ER
Tyrosine Hydroxylase
Catecholamines
Epinephrine (Adrenalin) & Norepinephrine

Fight or Flight Response

2. Adrenal Cortex Cell

ACTH
Nucleus
cAMP
Gene
XXXX
mRNA
ER
21-Hydroxylase
Steroids
Cortisol

General Adaptation Syndrome

Ref: The Psychology of Mind Body Healing by Ernest Lawrence Rossi

Habits for Responding to Feelings

"We forget first what we learnt last!"

We are creatures of habit and as a result of this we can lose awareness of what we are doing and how we respond. If you have decided to change then you will have to break your habits and put new behaviours in their place. For many people this can be hard and when things get difficult they may well slip back into their old habits. This is fine because "we forget first what we learnt last!"

To change your habits you need to become aware of them and the following exercise may help you get a handle on some of your beliefs about the nature of anger/sadness/happiness/fear. It is on these beliefs that your habits are based. Read the following items in a state of relaxed concentration, and allow yourself to honestly fill in the blanks with your reactions. If you need more space, use some note-paper

1.   A time when I really felt _____ at another human being was:

(insert emotion)

2.   At that time I chose to :

3.   As I remember that experience now I feel :

4.   If I had allowed my _____ to be reflected in my body and in my voice in a manner that was absolutely uncensored, I imagine that I would have:

5.   The _____ that I ever recall seeing anybody be was:

6.   When I witnessed him or her being that _____, I felt:

7.   When my mother was _____, she tended to:

8.   When my father was _____, he tended to

9.   It seems to me that I automatically associate _____ with (choose all that apply):

a. Power
b. Good
c. Bad
d. Productivity
e. Masculinity

f. Pain
g. Aliveness
h. Excitement
i. Darkness
j. Creativity
k. Harm

Add your own responses:
l.
m

There is no need for your to be frightened or cautious about acknowledging your beliefs/habits. Doing so does not imply that you need to change anything. Think through the validity of these beliefs or habits for you at this stage of your life, remembering that a habitual response, which made sense when it was formed, may have little value in your life as you currently experience it.

You might want to repeat the same exercise with other emotions such as sadness, fear and joy.

The poem 'If' by Kipling might also be considered as a useful description of a person who manages change effectively:

If

If you can keep your head when all about you
Are losing theirs and blaming it on you;
If you can trust yourself when all men doubt you,
But make allowance for their doubting too;
If you can wait and not be tired by waiting,
Or, being lied about, don't deal in lies,
Or, being hated, don't give way to hating,
And yet don't look too good, nor talk too wise;

If you can dream - and not make dreams your master;
If you can think - and not make thoughts your aim;
If you can meet with triumph and disaster
And treat those two imposters just the same;
If you can bear to hear the truth you've spoken
Twisted by knaves to make a trap for fools,
Or watch the things you gave your life to broken,
And stoop and build 'em up with wornout tools;

If you can make one heap of all your winnings
And risk it on one turn of pitch-and-toss,
And lose, and start again at your beginnings
And never breath a word about your loss;
If you can force your heart and nerve and sinew
To serve your turn long after they are gone,
And so hold on when there is nothing in you
Except the Will which says to them: "Hold on."

If you can talk with crowds and keep your virtue,
Or walk with kings - nor lose the common touch;
If neither foes nor loving friends can hurt you;
If all men count with you, but none too much;
If you can fill the unforgiving minute
With sixty seconds' worth of distance run -
Yours is the Earth and everything that's in it,
And - which is more - you'll be a Man my son!

References

Introduction
[1] Martin Seligman - 'Learned Optimism' 1990 - Pocket Books
[2] Daniel Goleman – 'Emotional Intelligence'1996 - Bloomsbury
[3] Howard Cutter – 'The Art of Happiness'
[4] Joe Griffin – 'Human Givens' 2003 – HG Publishing
[5] Aaron Beck – 'Cognitive Therapy and Emotional Disorders' – Penguin - 1991
[6] E.F. Schumacher – 'Small is Beautiful' Abacus 1973
[7] Ricardo Semler – 'Maverick' Arrow 1994
[8] Dalai Lama – 'The Art of Happiness' – Coronet Books 1998
[9] Argyle – 'The Psychology of Interpersonal Behaviour' – Penguin - 1994
[10] Moshe Feldenkrais – 'The Potent Self' – HarperSanFrancisco - 1985
[11] Cicely Berry – 'Voice and the Actor' Harrap London - 1979
[12] C Stanislawski – 'An Actor Prepares' Faber 1977
[13] Gerard Egan - "The Skilled Helper" Brooks/Cole - 1994
[14] Dr Michael Yapko - "Breaking the Patterns of Depression" – Broadway Books 1997
[15] Gerard Egan - "The Skilled Helper" Brooks/Cole - 1994

Emotions
[1] Richard D Carson - 'Taming your Gremlin' – HarperPerennial 1990

Values
[1] Dr Michael Yapko "Breaking the Patterns of Depression" – Broadway Books - 1997
[2] Gerard Egan "The Skilled Helper" Brooks/Cole - 1994
[3] Jim Collins – 'Built to Last' – 1990 – Century Business
[4] Adapted from "Breaking the Patterns of Depression" Broadway Books - 1997

Boundaries
[1] Adapted from the work of Dr Michael Yapko – "Breaking the Patterns of Depression"Broadway Books - 1997

Optimist Or Pessimist
[1] Martin Seligman – 'Learned Optimism' 1990 - Pocket Books

PEOPLE SKILLS

Communicating Effectively
[1] Napoleon Hill – 'Think and Grow Rich' - 1999 – Wilshire Book Co.

Developing Effective Communication Skills
[1] Bert Decker – 'How To Communicate Effectively' 1988 – Kogan Page
[2] Daniel Goleman – 'Emotional Intelligence'1996 - Bloomsbury
[3] Daniel Goleman – 'Emotional Intelligence'1996 - Bloomsbury
[4] Daniel Goleman – 'Emotional Intelligence'1996 - Bloomsbury
[5] Daniel Goleman – 'Emotional Intelligence'1996 - Bloomsbury
[6] Argyle – 'The Psychology of Interpersonal Behaviour' – Penguin - 1994
[7] Cialdini – 'Influence' Allyn & Bacon - 2001

8 Argyle – 'The Psychology of Interpersonal Behaviour' – Penguin - 1994
9 Kristin Linklater – 'Freeing the Natural Voice' - 2006
10 Cicely Berry – 'Voice and the Actor' Harrap London - 1979
11 Moshe Feldenkrais – 'The Potent Self' – HarperSanFrancisco - 1985
12 Stephen Covey – '7 Habits of Highly Effective People' – Simon & Schuster 1993
13 Argyle – 'The Psychology of Interpersonal Behaviour' – Penguin - 1994

Posture and Movement
1 Moshe Feldenkrais – 'The Potent Self' – HarperSanFrancisco - 1985
2 F.M. Alexander – The Alexander Technique Feldenkrais –
3 W.Reich – 'Character Analysis' - 1974
4 Alexander Lowen – 'Bioenergetics' – Penguin - 1975
5 Reich – 'Character Analysis' - 1974

The Energy Factor
1 Bert Decker – 'You Have To Be Believed To Be Heard' – Audiotape 1992
2 Whitworth, Kimsey-House, Sandahl 'Co-Active Coaching' – Davis-Black 1998
3 Gerard Egan "The Skilled Helper" Brooks/Cole - 1994

Words, non-words, the Pause and Silence
1 Jack Black – 'Mindstore' - 2007
2 Anthony Robbins – 'Awaken the Giant Within' - 2001
3 Zeus & Skiffington – 'Coaching at Work' – McGraw Hill Book Co. - 2000

Self-development of the Emotional Centre
1 Bert Decker – 'How To Communicate Effectively' 1988 – Kogan Page
2 Buscaglia 'The Art of Being Fully Human' - Audiotape
3 Bert Decker – 'How To Communicate Effectively' 1988 – Kogan Page
4 Dr Maxwell Maltz – 'Psycho-Cybernetics' – Wilshire Book Company 1960
5 Dr Maxwell Maltz – 'Psycho-Cybernetics' – Wilshire Book Company 1960
6 Adler &Heather - 'NLP in 21 Days' – Piatkus 1999
7 Myles Downney - 'Effective Coaching' – Target 1999

Emotional Centre and Emotional Intelligence
1 Daniel Goleman – 'Emotional Intelligence'1996 - Bloomsbury
2 Daniel Goleman – 'Emotional Intelligence'1996 - Bloomsbury
3 Bert Decker – 'How To Communicate Effectively' 1988 – Kogan Page
4 Dr Maxwell Maltz – 'Psycho-Cybernetics' – Wilshire Book Company 1960

The Observing Self
1Arthur J. Deikman, M.D. – "The Observing Self – Mysticism and Psychotherapy" Beacon Press 1982

BIBLIOGRAPHY

TITLE	AUTHOR	Year & Publisher
The Work We Were Born To Do	Nick Williams	1998
Take Yourself To The Top	Laura Berman Fortang	
Coaching For Performance	John Whitmore	1992
Co-Active Coaching	Whitworth, Kimsey-House,	1998 Davis-Black
Effective Coaching	Myles Downey	1999 Target
Success Through A Positive Mental Attitude	N Hill, W Clement Stone	1990 Thorson
Take Control Of Your Own Career	Barbara Buffton	
Unlocking your Potential	Dr Peter Marshall	
NLP in 21 Days	Adler and Heather	1998 Piatkus
An Introduction to NLP	J. O'Connor & J. Seymour	1990 Mandala
Coaching at Work	Zeus & Skiffington	2000 McGrawHill,
7 Habits of Highly Effective People	Stephen Covey	1999 Simon & Schuster
Awaken the Giant Within	Anthony Robbins	
Goals	Zig Ziglar	Audiotape
You Have To Be Believed To Be Heard	Bert Decker	1992
Work as a Spiritual Practise	Lewis Richmond	1999 Piatkus
What Matters Most	Hyrum W Smith	2000 Simon & Schuster
Think and Grow Rich	Napoleon Hill	1999 Wilshire Book s.
Team Roles at Work	M. Belbin	1993 Butterworth
The Essential Fromm	Erich Fromm	1995 Constable & Company
To Have Or To Be	Erich Fromm	1979 Abacus
The Art Of Listening	Erich Fromm	1994 Constable
The Art Of Loving	Erich Fromm	1995 Thorsons
The Art of Happiness	Dalai Lama - H Cutler	1998 Hodder & Stoughton
The Observing Self	Arthur J Deikman	1982 Beacon Press
The Tao of Pooh	Benjamin Hoff	1982 Methuen
The Tao Te Ching	Lao Tzu	2002 Watkins
The Prophet	Kahil Gibran	1972 Heinemann
The Potent Self	Moshe Feldenkrais	1992 HarperSanFrancisco
Awareness Through Movement	Moshe Feldenkrais	1972 Arkana

The Art of Living

Structural Fitness	John L Stirk	1988 Elm Tree Books
Bodysense	Sue Luby	
Voice and the Actor	Cicely Berry	1979: Harrap & London
Freeing the Natural Voice	C. Linklater	1976: Drama Publishers
Stanislavsky on the Art of the Stage	D. Magarshack	1950 Faber & Faber
T'ai Chi Ch'uan	Sophia Delza	1978 Cornerstone Library
The Alexander Technique	J. Leibowitz	Piatkus
Flexibility Training	J. McNaught Davis	1991 Partridge Press
The Actor's Body	Ross Brittleton	1999
The Silent Way	Galeb Gattegno	1986 Educational Solutions
The Generation of Wealth	Galeb Gattegno	1986 Educational Solutions
Who Moved My Cheese	Dr Spencer Johnson	
Character Analysis	Willhelm Reich	1969 Vision
Andrew Carnegie,	An Autobigraphy	Andrew Carnegie
What We May Be	Piero Ferrucci	1982
The Skilled Helper	Gerard Egan	1994 Brooks/Cole
Healing Emotions	Daniel Goleman	1997 Shambhala
Small is Beautiful	E.F. Schumacher	1973 Abacus

R oss Brittleton is a coach, physical therapist, psychotherapist, trainer and educator. His innovative, creative and imaginative methods reflect over 25 years experience gained from working in a wide variety of work environments and learning the most up to date methods available.

T hrough his work in the fields of business, health, education and the arts he places the ability to communicate and manage our lives effectively as the cornerstone of training in both personal and professional settings. By allowing people to "do" he believes they learn far more effectively. Over the years he has developed ways of working that allow people to develop their communication, organisational, planning and personal development skills.

H e has discovered that research has repeatedly shown that emotions, conditioning, the use or mis-use of our natural abilities and the level of skills we possess are at the heart of all actions and for all working relationships to be truly successful people need to know how to manage all of these effectively which allows a relationship of trust to be built.

H is first commitment is to people and using technology so that it enhances a person's life. He works with individuals or groups to help them to develop all the skills they will need to live and work more effectively in an ever-changing world. Ross offers a wide range of training and the areas he covers include

Coaching – Self & Others	Managing Change
Presentation Skills	Stress Management
Work/Life Balance	Assertiveness Skills
Developing Emotional Intelligence	Values Audit for Businesses
Time Management	Effective Communication
Developing Self-Confidence	Work S.M.A.R.T.E.R.
An Ethical Approach To Selling	

For details on coaching, counselling, any of the above courses or the range of work that Ross does you can look at **www.elementals.net** or email **info@elementals.net**. Copies of this book can also be ordered directly from Ross by contacting him at the email address above.